MENTAL AND EMOTIONAL HOUSE CLEANING AND MANAGEMENT

MENTAL AND EMOTIONAL HOUSE CLEANING AND MANAGEMENT

Manual for discovery, freedom, and life

BY SAM NAPIER

XULON PRESS

Xulon Press
2301 Lucien Way #415
Maitland, FL 32751
407.339.4217
www.xulonpress.com

Paperback ISBN-13: 978-1-66286-117-8
Ebook ISBN-13: 978-1-66286-118-5

TABLE OF CONTENTS

Credits

I t would truly be impossible to give proper recognition to all the people that have influenced my life through their written or verbal wisdom. I must say, I also owe a debt of gratitude to those who made it necessary for me to search so desperately for answers just to mentally and emotionally survive. Without them, I may never have found the treasures that changed my life so completely and that enrich my life still today.

Everything I am able to share in this book is the result of a lifetime of mental and emotional extremes. It was a path of unguided thoughts and emotions that led to a point of brokenness and despair. It is also the result of a life of mental and emotional discovery, freedom, and life with endless possibilities.

Part of the responsibility of learning such valuable life lessons is sharing them. Such lessons are never meant to stop with the person that learns from them. They are a universal map for the successful journey of any individual person.

The pain of being at the so called "end of your rope" makes you feel like no one understands what you're going through, and you may feel all alone in the struggle. I can assure you, there is at least one person who can relate to your pain or brokenness, no matter how extreme.

I give all credit for the information in this book to the One who gave a helping hand to me. He gave me the means to clean and maintain a mental and emotional home the way it was meant to be.

Introduction

Everyone's home needs a good cleaning once in a while, especially if it is just let go. Sometimes it may deteriorate and be damaged in a way that it needs a total rebuild. Also, a home sitting on a weak foundation is subject to undesirable movement and shifting caused by any storm or influence that is strong enough to cause an unwanted move. Movement or shifting that happens gradually and unnoticed can eventually cause the need for a total rebuild.

Even if we think we are keeping things in order, we can still get piled up with needless things that just take up space and get in the way. We may have to take extreme action, after we allow toxic wastes to have an intolerable effect on everything and everyone around us, and especially ourselves. It's when we gradually allow ourselves to adapt to small, unacceptable conditions, that we eventually find ourselves in an unbearable state of affairs.

A good cleaning, and management, require special tools and equipment and commitment. The same goes for our mind and emotions. No matter what condition you find your thoughts and emotions in presently, you can benefit from the age-old truths laid out in these pages. I can personally declare they are powerful and effective.

This isn't a prolonged clinical explanation of several cases of thought and emotional management. Let's face it! When we need useful direction in thought and emotional change and management, we need it now!

This book is focused on immediate, clear, and proven effectiveness. It gives a practical and real method of mental and emotional house cleaning and management that can, and should be, put into practice today. All who wish to free themselves of the pain and torment of mental and emotional adjustments gone awry, or just simply desire to learn the life changing direction that enables proper management of thoughts and emotions, will find a path of discovery, freedom and life, by following the guidelines given in this book.

A mental or emotional adjustment is the condition we find ourselves in as the result of any influence which is strong enough to cause a change in our present mental or emotional condition. If we don't have a solid foundation of mental and emotional guidelines to keep us in a condition that promotes our wellbeing we could be forced into a toxic, painful, unmanageable condition by unmanaged adjustments. It is very possible to have the pain and misery of unmanaged adjustments effect our daily life for many years, even a lifetime. Any one of us can experience circumstances, at times, that overwhelm us and cause unwelcome adjustments. That need not be the case any longer. Please continue with me on this journey of a lifetime.

SECTION ONE:

DISCOVERY

Chapter One:

A New Resident

New and Vulnerable

Think of a new, orderly, clean home, out in a vast wilderness that has a new resident who knows nothing of the dangers that may be present in the surrounding area. Doors and windows being left open, all the time, would leave the dwelling totally vulnerable to any invader that might venture in. Being vulnerable and inexperienced, the resident would have to adjust to whatever changes the invaders may happen to make to his residence. What an unpredictable, chaotic, position to be in!

Now think of each one of us when we were newly born babes. We found ourselves a resident of a new home (body, mind, and emotions) that possibly hadn't been excessively influenced one way or the other. We began our occupancy with all the doors open; to any sound, taste, sight, feeling, or smell that would happen, by chance, to influence us one way or the other.

We automatically adjusted, by yielding to whatever thought or emotion that may have been awakened, by random circumstances or people. We had no idea what lurked in the surrounding wilderness or how to guard against any unwanted influences. At that point, we were not capable of having any safeguards in place. What a predicament!

We were at the mercy of whatever thought or emotion could be generated by a world of diverse influences, good or bad. At that time of vulnerability, our dwelling could be shifted or drastically changed by any influence that was strong enough.

More than likely, we continued that automatic, unmanaged, or natural mode of adapting to life. The lack of management; Could have led to having an unstable, chaotic, damaged, or very painful mental and emotional dwelling place; It could have led to a haphazard, tolerable, semi-managed mental and emotional dwelling place; It could also have led to an attempted withdrawal from all possible influences, because of a distorted adjustment of fear.

It is very important to understand what an adjustment is; A mental or emotional condition which is the result of something or someone's influence upon us which is strong enough to change our current mental and emotional state, is an adjustment. Life, as it is, minute by minute, exposes all of us to random circumstances which can influence our adjustments, minor or major, one way or the other, for our benefit or to our detriment. Not knowing how to manage our adjustments can allow toxic adjustments to remain in place to have a negative effect on our daily lives.

The condition of our past adjustments that are still influencing our daily lives can be called the condition of our life's foundation. We may have unknowingly formed any number of attitudes or thought patterns that make up our default mode of functioning in daily life. This random adoption of adjustments could have worked against us or in our favor.

Our default mode, could be very restrictive and binding if built on selfishness, fear, hate, pride, stubbornness, divisiveness, depression, or timidity. These are some of the most natural adjustments to fall into. In other words, they are invaders. They never ask for control. They take and take until they control our thoughts and emotions. They are toxic, destructive invaders that must be evicted as soon as they are detected. The enslavement of such distorted thoughts and emotions creates division and disruption around us and within us.

Some parents or guardians may have protected many young ones from unwanted and extreme influences, which helped them mature with a solid foundation to some degree. Everyone has adjusted in a way to help them adapt to everyday life in the best way they knew how, and we all continue to adjust because an everchanging world requires it of us. The big question is, are the adjustments making us stronger and wiser, or are they doing damage?

Questions to Ponder:

1. Can you remember something that happened to you or around you when you were a child that raises the same emotions today as when it happened?

2. Is it an uplifting emotion or an enslaving emotion you would like to be free from?

You Can Choose

We all need to develop sufficient abilities to evaluate our own thoughts and emotions. We must learn to choose between those that are worthy of acceptance and those that are not. We must learn how to discard the unworthy ones and retain or create worthy ones and build on them. Begin to believe that is possible! You will see the proof of it as you progress through this journey of discovery, freedom, and life.

The ultimate goal of creating a life foundation of peace and truth that grows brighter each day is within reach for all of us. It just requires the correct tools, materials, focus in the right direction, and commitment. One step at a time will take you out of the darkness of chaotic shadows to the light of day to build an unshakable foundation as you follow "The Daily Walk" described near the end of this book. The progression of the understanding laid out in this book will offer the most benefit if followed from the beginning.

Good adjustments may seem totally out of reach when we get bomb shelled with extreme negative influences. Severe damage is possible if we do not have an unshakable foundation. We can easily begin feeling and thinking like a victim. Feelings of fear, anger, suspicion, selfishness, self-pity, resentment, and many other unwanted emotional intruders can be awakened within us.

Those intruders work to poison our thoughts and create a toxic, negative environment in our mind. That toxic condition fuels the fires of runaway emotions. It may seem natural to fall into this trap because it is so easy to go in the direction we have been conditioned to.

Questions to Ponder:

1. Is there something you dread happening, because if it did happen, it would ruin your day before it even began?

2. Do you think, that doom and gloom feeling, has more authority over you than it should have?

Task Masters

Our thoughts and emotions will go wherever they are allowed to go, or they will go where they are directed to go.

That can be very detrimental, or it can be very uplifting and enlightening, depending on who or what is doing the directing. Our thoughts and emotions are like play dough in someone else's hands, if we submit to the random influences of circumstances or other people or our own misguided notions. That could make us slaves to merciless task masters.

The influences that cause the need for mental and emotional adjustment, however minor or severe, can strengthen or weaken us, overwhelm us, or we can shut down our mental and emotional adjustments, which is never good. Good adjustments create confidence, peace, joy, love, good health, and all the qualities that lift us higher than we were before. Every need for an adjustment is an opportunity to rise higher or succumb to deeper slavery to intruder thoughts and emotions. We can choose which. Yes, we most certainly can!

If not checked with the proper safeguards, thoughts and emotions can run amuck and create unstable, uncomfortable, or unbearable conditions. When negative influences build up, we may find ourselves hoping nothing happens to push us over the edge. That attitude is the product of thoughts and feelings that go something like:

A. Why do these things happen to me?
B. When are things going to change?
C. Why does life have to be so miserable?

Questions to Ponder:

1. Is there a certain situation you enter on a regular basis that triggers a particular thought or feeling automatically?

2. When that happens, do you feel in control of your thoughts and emotions, or do you think you are on autopilot?

Temporary Relief

A vacation, a weekend full of partying, or the many other attempts at temporarily managing our unwanted and enslaving thoughts and emotions, helps us keep going another week, or even just another day. The statement, "It is what it is", sometimes excuses us from taking responsibility for any kind of meaningful adjustment or action. We need to always remember; when circumstances or people seem beyond our control, our own thoughts and emotions are not.

We can get so distracted, with unintentional, and sometimes even damaging thoughts and emotions that our everyday activities may seem difficult and unmanageable. To receive any thought or emotion, as a guest, is like riding on a wagon pulled by a team of out of control, wild horses, without reins in our hands.

Whatever condition you may find your mental and emotional home in currently, there is hope of thorough cleaning and management. The preparation, plan, and "The Daily Walk," as explained in this book, are all designed to meet you wherever you are and guide you to a much better place of freedom and life!

Questions to Ponder:

1. Do you rely on any particular activity during the weekend to get you through the next week?

2. Do you feel trapped in a never-ending cycle?

Never Meant to Operate on Autopilot

We are not born with an automatic, efficient, capable, and peaceful manner of managing thoughts and emotions. That is something we must learn, or we will just gradually become the product of unmanaged thoughts and emotions. It becomes like trying to build a foundation by unknowingly throwing unworthy material under our house to try to hold it up. Nothing seems to fall in its proper place. It also feels like wherever we try to gain a solid stance is always shifting.

Our own thoughts can be our most brutal enemies. They can create emotions that torture and torment and grow more potent when and if we act on them. If we affirm a negative thought or emotion by a careless statement or action, they only become stronger. Some examples of negative and damaging statements that start to gradually create toxic mental and emotional conditions are:

1. I can't do anything right!
2. I can't seem to get it. My brain's not working today!
3. I'll never understand!
4. Anyone could do better than I can!
5. No one seems to understand.
6. They don't care about me.
7. I can't seem to help myself.
8. I will get even.
9. I can't trust anyone.
10. I don't know how long I can keep this up.

The direction our mind takes in thought is strongly influenced by our emotions. Our emotions are turned in one direction or the other by our thoughts. Sounds like a recipe for chaos, doesn't it? Let me give you an example:

If someone walked right up and punched you in the nose, you would first be shocked, then maybe angry. You may start thinking what to do about it if you don't just act on impulse. Then, even a month or so after the incident, you start thinking about it again. The same anger could be aroused and maybe even more thoughts of how you could have handled it differently.

That mismanagement of thoughts and emotions could leave you trapped in the same cycle for years, even a lifetime. It makes a big difference which one you allow to dominate (thoughts or emotions). Your mind is a powerful force. If it is directed improperly or just allowed to run free, it can create thoughts and emotions that make life unbearable. Just think of what can happen if you learn how to manage thoughts and emotions and find freedom while creating an unshakable foundation.

If managed properly, our thought and emotional home can be an unshakable, peaceful, friendly, and productive place that we can enjoy. The mental and emotional riches that we may have thought out of reach or unattainable (love, joy, peace, wisdom, understanding) will become possible, regardless of our position or condition in life.

You can, and must, take responsibility for your thoughts and emotions if you would have stability and peace. It begins simply with your thought or decision to take ownership of where you live (your house of thoughts and emotions).

Questions to Ponder:

1. Have you ever acted or spoken like you were under the control of a strong thought or emotion beyond your control?

2. Did that create a desperation to do something to get yourself under control?

Owner or Renter

If you don't see yourself as the "responsible party" for your mind and emotions, you may unknowingly have the attitude that you are just renting and someone else is responsible for the upkeep and maintenance. You may have fallen into the trap of thinking; "life is what it is, and I have to go with the flow." That is like being on the freeway of life and not choosing to put your hands on the steering wheel.

There is a real danger, if you don't take responsibility for your own thoughts and emotions. There could be a very dominating, deceptive, nagging, and painfully disruptive thought or emotion, caused by unpredictable circumstances; create a life changing adjustment, that has a detrimental effect on your welfare, if not managed properly. The rules of occupancy don't allow you to focus on unwanted occupants and just tell them to leave. The more you are focused on any unwanted thought or emotion, the stronger they become. It is important to know how to reject and avoid undesirables, no matter how strong they are.

Some of the adjustments you have adapted to, may seem permanent. A common way of thinking is "it's just the way I am" or "these are the cards life has dealt me and I have no choice." Those are simply thoughts and emotions that have been given authority they shouldn't have.

Adjustments are only permanent if you allow them to be. The power of any distorted adjustment can be crippling or disabling. That binding power of intrusive adjustments can and must be erased.

Questions to ponder:

1. Do you think you are the product of past circumstances?

2. Do you feel like you are carrying any unwanted mental and emotional baggage from the past?

Chapter Two:

Inspect Your Foundation

Foundational Integrity

The ego (selfish, prideful, stubborn, and fearful of the unfamiliar) hates to give up familiar adjustments. We all seem to define who we are by the adjustments we have had to make. That, can lead to a miserable existence, especially if the dominating adjustments are negative. Remember, the foundation our thought and emotional house sits on can be unsteady and unpredictable today but doesn't have to stay that way.

We can even put on such a perfect front each day, trying to hide our misery and struggle from the world, that we begin to believe we are perfectly safe from our misery. The truth is, that misery, no matter how deep it is buried inside us, can create toxic thoughts and emotions that totally surprise us at times. It also becomes harder to recognize the truth when we have any distorted adjustments that are having a toxic effect on our daily lives.

The key to clearing away the effects of a toxic foundation and begin creating a solid foundation, at any point in life, no matter how extreme the past adjustments have been, is, to not define who you are, by the adjustments you have had to make. It is possible to erase the influence of past adjustments to be free to build a new unshakeable foundation.

Extreme circumstances, can leave you unable to adjust effectively at the time they occur, so you push the thought of them away to the closet of our mind, without any emotional attachment to them. That is like residing in a house with no foundation, and not acknowledging when it shifts under the pressure of life and circumstances, a guarantee for future collapse.

When that closet door somehow is opened by a trigger word or flash of a memory, a flood of mixed, chaotic, unmanageable thoughts and emotions, can make their way to the surface. That can leave you puzzled, and doing damage control, if you are unable to contain the influences. Think of the influence of a full closet!

Change your perspective, and gain clearer understanding, and freedom to create. Don't allow influences of random, uncontrolled circumstances and people define who you are any longer. You are so much more than that! Let's begin to uncover the remarkable you that has been hidden behind all those adjustments or lack thereof.

Questions to Ponder:

1. Have you ever had a strong, impulsive thought or emotion surprise you because it had no apparent reason to spring up?

2. Do you easily bring those intruding thoughts and emotions under control?

The Deceptive Ego

You have to resist and replace the thoughts your ego may have inspired from past adjustments to be able to make an unbiased, rational decision. A thought to focus on, that may help overcome an unhelpful ego would be:

> "I need to do this for my own welfare, peace of mind, and for those around me!"

Your "decision" is all it takes to begin taking ownership of your thoughts and emotions and building an unshakable life foundation. This is not just something, we all, need to do. It is something, we all, *must* do, if we don't want to live in the unmanaged condition of random thoughts and emotions inspired by chance, the influence of someone or something else, or our own misdirection. Our lives are meant to be so much more than that!

The journey described throughout this book, is meant to ultimately, bring you to taking "The Daily Walk" which combines the truths revealed throughout this book. That will daily bring you to valuable places of discovery, freedom and life. It is very important to understand the progression of this journey from the beginning. If followed sincerely, faithfully, from the beginning, this journey will truly be transforming and unending. The joy of being in the position to grow into who you were meant to be, only gets better with each step you take each day. Here listed are some of the proven benefits of carefully progressing through the journey described in this book and then faithfully taking "The Daily Walk":

1. Discover that you are truly not defined by the adjustments of the past unless you allow it.
2. Discover the part of you that has been overshadowed.
3. Learn the steps to victory over internal struggles.
4. Experience true freedom from the shackles of the past.
5. Learn to walk the path of wisdom that lifts you higher.
6. See the truth that illuminates the path of wisdom.
7. Learn to receive and give unconditional love. (Yes, it is possible!)
8. Learn to live with the peace of mind that surpasses all understanding. (Again, yes, it is possible!)

Break the ego chains that may be preventing you from seeing the need to take this journey. Begin with victory over what could be a selfish, prideful, stubborn, and fearful ego (and it always is). Accept a pattern of thoughts that points you in the direction you want to go. Don't get me wrong, acceptance of a productive thought pattern is a means to get started in a good direction but is not the entirety of the journey drawn out in this book.

Some thoughts worth accepting:

1. "I need to look at this with an open mind."
2. "If this can help me have a better life, I need to give it a chance."
3. "If this plan can help me develop a positive outlook, I need to give it all my attention."
4. "If this journey will lift me out of the rut, I'm in, I will accept this challenge."
5. "If there is something more than existing, struggling, working, and dying, I'm in all the way!"
6. "I seek an unshakable foundation of life."
7. "I need to know the purpose of my life and who I am meant to be,"

Questions to Ponder:

1. Have you ever had the thought, "you can't teach old dogs, new tricks"?

2. How has that manner of thinking served you so far? (Remove the boundaries of your thinking and you remove the limitations of your life!)

Section Two:

Finding Freedom

Chapter Three:

Living Proof

We All Begin Somewhere

I would like to give you the example of my own life, which has been filled with extremely unmanaged adjustments that were brought on by excessively merciless and damaging circumstances. The point I want to make, is, no matter how deeply you may be imbedded in the extreme, distorted adjustments of the past, you must not let them define you. The recovery, from such a life of extreme and distorted adjustments, is an example of what can happen when help is accepted from the proper extended hand. The hand that leads us to a higher place than we are currently, is always worthy of acceptance.

Questions to Ponder:

1. Once a victim of damaging circumstances, are you always that victim?

(As you know by now, daily life is one lesson after the other. What you carry forward from each lesson can make you wiser and stronger or make you weak, unsure, and doubtful until you feel and think like a perpetual victim. You may not even remember what started the toxic path of thinking and feeling like a victim. Do not accept that deception as your identity any longer!)

2. Do you have a choice of what you carry forward each day?

(Many times, if the thought or feeling is severe enough, they seem impossible to leave behind. If they are all you know, they can take a position of authority in defining who you are. The good thing is, no matter how long you have been under the authority of intruding thoughts and emotions, you can remove their authority and toxicity with something that is much stronger. Continue this journey, and you will have it.)

My Story

My life began on a small farm in southeastern Kentucky. Isolation and poverty seemed to govern my childhood as far back as I can remember. There were no playmates or fun times, just isolation and whatever my imagination could muster up. For more years than I care to recall, when I was a child, the only times I was given any thought or human interaction was when I was told to get up, hurry and eat breakfast, eat all my dinner, go to bed, or when I was the recipient of discipline.

The only ray of sunshine throughout my early years was a mother that worked endlessly to provide for a family that grew to nine children. Her devotion, love, and commitment never wavered in her efforts to put three meals on the table every day, keep us in clean clothes, and work in the fields each day as well. She also grew a huge garden each year which she managed to stretch through the summers and winters by canning and freezing food.

Her show of love and occasional words of affection, though she rarely had time to divert her priceless attention toward me, was the one thing that kept me from being overwhelmed by the mental and emotional turmoil of my daily life. There was very little time left over for human interaction when everyone came home after working the fields all day.

Questions to Ponder:

1. What can you learn when you are surrounded by darkness?

2. How important is the smallest flicker of light when you are emersed in darkness?

The Real Beginning of Mental and Emotional Turmoil

The day finally came when I was old enough to help in the fields. I felt like I had graduated to usefulness. What a great feeling, being among people. I don't know what was more painful; not being around people all day every day, or being around people that never talked to me and never thought I had anything useful to say; not that I had developed any communication abilities.

No one ever saw the need to help me develop any ability to communicate effectively. This same lack of communication development went right alongside emotional turmoil which continued without improvement well into my teen years. I adjusted by finding great satisfaction in doing the best job I could, in all I was given to do, just to be told occasionally as someone walked by, "good job". I was no more than a pet receiving a treat. That seemed to be the extent of human interaction in the fields until I was moved into more challenging tasks sometime later.

I was totally at the mercy of random circumstances and good or bad interactions with people, because I had no foundation of mental and emotional growth or thoughtful adjustment capability. Of course, I didn't know this at that time. Neither did I have any experience interacting with or responding to other people in any way that would promote any communication beyond the very basic acknowledgment of presence. Any depth of interaction with anyone, always left me to later feel inadequate and beneath anyone I might encounter in the future. My self-confidence was nonexistent.

Every encounter brought on feelings of emptiness, inadequacy, sadness, and a deep desire to discover what I was missing that everyone else seemed to have. Those same feelings became deeply imbedded as my school years passed.

Questions to Ponder:

1. Have you ever found yourself mentally or emotionally unable to meet the moment you were in?

2. How would it feel to not have any foundational capability to manage any human interaction?

Intense Turmoil

Working all day; in the tobacco patches, corn fields, or hay fields, was the most I could look forward to each day. Having fun was something that was unknown to me. All too often, I spent days at a time not speaking to anyone and no one speaking to me. Often, I felt I was invisible. I came to enjoy being alone much more than being around people that treated me like I wasn't there. That was odd, simply for the fact I grew up in a family of nine children.

All of us seemed to be subjected to similar treatment that varied to some degree. My isolation, lack of communication, neglect, emptiness, and inner turmoil seemed to overshadow my ability to observe most of what happened to anyone else.

Questions to Ponder:

1. Can the presence of others, without interaction, fulfill our most basic social need?

2. What do you think the absence of fun times does to the mental and emotional condition?

Automatic Adjustments Gone Sour

I spent many of my young years assisting my grandfather all summer long when he bailed hay on our farm or for our neighbors. My responsibility was to ride on the hay bailer and get his attention when a bail didn't get tied correctly before it hit the ground. Yelling over the noise of farm machinery wasn't the easiest thing to do after sitting in a mind-numbing position all day breathing dust and diesel fumes. After some time, I felt like I was a part of that machinery, just to be used and discarded when my usefulness wore out.

There were many times I could not yell over the noise of the equipment and get his attention before the bail hit the ground in a loose, untied mess. It seemed that all I ever heard from my grandfather was a flurry of angry, degrading comments. He never displayed any signs of understanding or compassion or love. Not that I was the least bit familiar with those qualities of human communication at that time. I felt like I was just another tool. His constant insults and anger brought on constant feelings of guilt, inadequacy, and shame that didn't leave me until many years later.

Sometimes the verbal abuse would escalate to physical abuse, which resulted in constant feelings of anger, hatred, fear, and guilt. These feelings dominated my daily existence until I learned how to disguise them, with a fake smile or false patience, while I fumed inside. What constant turmoil!

To add to that volcanic mental and emotional activity, my grandfather would complain to my dad about his displeasure with me and that brought on Dad's wrath. It didn't take Dad long to graduate from the use of the belt to the use of his fists. One day he felt the need to discipline me until he was out of breath and unable to punch any more. I was thankful he wasn't in very good shape.

Questions to Ponder:

1. Can we become a prisoner of life without being locked in a facility?

2. Can a person have hope of something better, even if there is no knowledge of what it might be, or how to achieve much of anything, just a strong desire?

An Instinct to Survive

My social experiences were almost nonexistent in my early years. Social interaction, fun, love, friendship, communication, support, and general instruction for living didn't seem to be a priority for our family. It seemed the goal was to just survive another day.

My goal each day progressed to trying to stay out of sight and out of mind. It seemed some sort of discipline came my way each day regardless of my efforts. I think I had become a scape goat. I adjusted by feeling I deserved the discipline, because I must be doing something wrong. Constant feelings of guilt and inferiority dominated my behavior and thoughts in every encounter.

Social, mental, and emotional development was left to chance. I think the lack of focus in those areas of development was evidence that my parents, and others I was associated with each day, were not taught those qualities themselves. They simply followed the same pattern for life they experienced their whole lives. Mom's occasional word of compassion, when she could divert her priceless attention from her mountain of responsibilities, is all that made me feel like I was alive.

These are not statements borne from a feeling of resentment, regret, or self-pity. They are simply the facts of my life. I knew I was empty, miserable, and hopeless. Sometimes I felt I was a helpless slave under the control of my constant feelings of anger, hatred, resentment, guilt, inferiority, and fear. I felt I was trapped in circumstances that doomed me to a short, hopeless, and miserable life if I didn't escape as soon as I could.

I made a plan to get out into the world after my high school years, to discover what I was missing and escape the misery. I think the pain of so many severely distorted adjustments and my desperation drove me more than bravery. I admit, I had a full closet of influences I didn't acknowledge because I was unable to adjust to them so I just pretended they didn't happen. That left me dragging a load of mental and emotional baggage which made me wonder if there was such a thing as normality.

I also admit, I didn't understand what bravery was in the least, at that time. As mentally and emotionally deprived and distorted as my condition had become, I was determined to discover who I really was, and what life had to offer, that I had never known before.

Questions to Ponder:

1. How would you feel going out into an unknown world with nothing to work with and no social skills?

2. Can you have any self-confidence if you haven't developed any idea of who you are?

A Search for Something Better

It seemed that the only way I could get out of my situation was to join the military, so I joined the Air Force. Those old feelings of guilt and inferiority seemed to stick with me. Whenever anything went wrong anywhere around me, I had an automatic "guilty" feeling spring up within me, as if I had caused it.

It wasn't easy living in an open barracks full of about forty other guys from all over the United States. Needless to say, my social skills were nonexistent. I had to rely on a simple, shy smile to get me through all social encounters. Working on a small Kentucky farm from daylight till dark, under slavish conditions, didn't lend itself to create any popular discussions. I wasn't armed with any other useful conversational knowledge or ability, so I did a lot of listening.

I had to really work hard at hiding my impatience, anger, resentment, fear, guilt, and social ignorance. My fear of appearing ignorant and my desperate need for people's approval made me retreat into a timidity and a feeling of dependency that drew people's sympathy more than real friendship. At that point in my life, the feeling of friendship was unknown to me.

I seemed to leave every social encounter feeling ashamed and humiliated and not knowing what to do about it. I had developed a social anxiety that seemed to control everything I said and did around people. I felt constantly exhausted from the emotional and mental turmoil that was part of my daily existence. Oh, what misery! I had no idea how to enjoy someone's company or be a joy to someone. Joy was unknown to me.

Questions to Ponder:

1.   Can you build on a foundation that doesn't exist?

2.   Where do you start if you don't know how to build a foundation, much less, know the need for one?

A Necessary Escape

The job situation was very awkward because everything I did required interaction with many other people. It was as if I was being placed in those positions purposefully to teach me how to relate to other people. I learned to just shut my emotions down because I didn't really know how to feel in most situations and that just seemed to take a lot of stress away. One problem with that was it left me empty and unable to initiate any kind of social interaction myself.

I learned, I could build a little self-confidence and ease the social stress by going to the gym every day. I worked out about four hours every day. My efforts to burn off the daily stress led me to work out until I was totally exhausted. Everywhere I went, it was necessary to relate to many other people. That caused constant stress.

I also found some relief in going to the local bars. Alcohol seemed to be a temporary safe haven for me at the time. Numbing the constant emotional and mental pain seemed to require ever increasing amounts of alcohol as time went on. Somehow, I knew that this was the wrong path, after a few years of throwing money away, recovering from many bad hangovers, constantly feeling guilty about wasting my life, and engaging in very unwise behavior, some of which I could not recall.

Questions to Ponder:

1. Can our escape become our main priority in life?

2. Is that an adjustment that has been given too much authority?

A Necessary Relationship

The experience I had over several years of developing short term relationships with young ladies left me thinking I would probably never be married. I felt even more hopeless and empty. Every time I met a young lady, my greatest fear was she would see through my false words and actions to see my real emptiness and ignorance. I couldn't stay in any relationship too long.

Then I met a young lady who had standards, confidence, and poise and on top of that she was beautiful. My interest was awakened. (After 42 years of marriage, two children, and many, many lessons in maturity and growth, I continue to be enrolled in the very challenging University of Life, currently working on a master's degree).

My social skills were more adequate than in the past, but much was still to be desired. Our relationship grew and we eventually married. A beautiful baby was born into our lives, and I really had no idea how to be a father. All I knew was I wanted a better life for our child than I had experienced. My old feelings of guilt and inadequacy were revived with force. I couldn't drown those feelings out by spending four hours in the gym or spending my nights at the local bar anymore. Those feelings were magnified by the lack of experience at my job and small paychecks.

Questions to Ponder:

1. Do circumstances adjust, in any way, to our tolerance level, automatically?

2. Is there a point of no return, concerning our ability to adjust, when passed?

The Crushing Blow

The social stress seemed to grow more intense. An office environment, which demanded constant social interaction mixed with many professionally developed personalities, left me feeling helpless and extremely inadequate.

Then, in the midst of my daily struggle, I received a call from my mom back in Kentucky. At that time, I was stationed 1,400 miles away. I was crushed by the news that one of my sisters had nearly died. All I could think about was that I was too far away to help her, and I shouldn't have left Kentucky. I fell straight into my usual self-blame game.

The guilt and inadequacy feelings took over my existence. The self-torturing thoughts bombarded my mind, mercilessly and constantly. A week later, I received another call, that a brother nearly lost his life. I had been weakened and worn, so severely from the previous call, that something happened to me that was different and extreme; I was broken.

Like a hammer could smash a clay pot, the overwhelming phone call took my sense of guilt and inadequacy past their limits and gave my mental and emotional condition a death blow. I sank to the floor of that little apartment a helpless, broken, tortured man. I couldn't talk on the phone, so my wife took it from my hand.

I could not recover from the empty, hopeless, broken, and miserable semblance of a human being that I had become. It felt like life was pouring out of my body every day. I didn't want to go to sleep at night due to the dread of waking up to resume the same miserable state of being, the next day. The pain seemed to have no end, and I couldn't do anything about it. My thoughts and emotions grew more extreme hour by hour, day by day. I accepted the thought that I had no hope of recovery. So, I made a plan to do the only thing I thought would end the extreme pain that had taken over my life.

I woke up the next Sunday morning and dropped my wife and daughter off at church. I explained that I wasn't feeling well, and I would pick them up after church. I went back to the apartment and set the stage to make it look like an accident. After a few minutes, I had a twelve-gage shotgun loaded with buckshot pointed at my chest.

I wanted to talk to God one last time. I had accepted the idea that Jesus Christ was my savior some years before but just to get my ticket to heaven. I put that thought on the shelf until needed. At that point in time, I felt God was a million miles away. I also thought I was too insignificant in the grand scheme of things for God to pay any attention to me. I ventured a short prayer anyway. I told God, "I put myself in your hands and if you don't change me completely right now, I will consider it your will that I leave this world, broken and hopeless."

Questions to Ponder:

1. Can your mental, emotional, and spiritual state all be broken at the same time?

- *"A joyful heart makes a cheerful face, but when the heart is sad, the spirit is broken."* Proverbs 15:3

2. Can you repair a broken spirit?

- *"The sacrifices of God are a broken spirit; A broken and contrite heart, God, you will not despise."* Psalms 51:17

The Helping Hand

I then reached for the trigger with my foot. I felt a hand grab my ankle and stop my foot. I looked, and saw no-one there. I tried again, and the same thing happened. At that moment, the best I can describe it, is, all the pain, guilt, emptiness, and hopelessness were lifted, right out of me. It felt like my spirit had been removed from my body, because I felt something being removed from the tips of my toes to the top of my head. I also felt when something was put back into me without the pain, hopelessness, and brokenness. I felt like a different person. Don't get me wrong, the way I began this journey, I truly hope is different for other people.

You may think, I have really gone off the deep end now, but I feel I must tell you what happened, the best I can. The truth is, no matter how low or broken you feel, there is always hope. God is absolutely real, and His love and goodness are never far away.

That moment, I was filled with a magnificent peace, freedom, and boldness. These were things, I had never felt before. I had no idea what extreme emotional and mental bondage and torment I had been in all my life until I knew this new freedom and peace. The new boldness seemed to replace the feelings of dependency, timidity, and self-doubt. For the first time ever, I felt like I was alive! Oh, the joy that was borne within me at that moment; I cannot describe! Joy was unknown to me, until that moment.

That moment, I was awakened to the reality of my spirit. I remember being taught about it in church a few years before, but now I knew the truth of it. I knew something fresh and good had just begun. I felt clean inside. I knew, at that moment, I was lifted from underneath all those distorted adjustments. I was awakened to the truth of having a spiritual door. I didn't understand what had just happened, but I knew, I had been given some things I had never known before, and if I wanted to keep them, I had better learn how. Little did I know at the time, that all these new qualities of life, came with the entrance of the divine nature of Christ into my heart (spirit).

Questions to Ponder:

1. Does your perception of yourself effect your perception of the world around you?

*   *"Or do you not know that your body is a temple of the Holy Spirit within you, whom you have from God, and that you are not your own? For you have been bought for a price: therefore, glorify God in your body."* 1 Corinthians 6:19-20

2. Do you think there is a place within you, beyond your awareness, that needs more than you have to give it?

*   *"He spoke another parable to them: "The kingdom of heaven is like leaven, which a woman took and hid in three sata of flour until it was all leavened."* Matthew 13:33.

(When you know, you have received the divine nature of Christ within your heart, you will grow in a strong desire, to know Him more.)

Chapter Four:

A New Perspective

Significance of the Gift

I picked up my wife and daughter after church that day. She has never known the details of that day until now. We have been married 42 years. The Lord has brought us through these past 42 years, teaching us many valuable lessons. Each one has made us more humble, wiser and thankful.

I feel this lesson of a second chance, is one I must share with all that are struggling with too many questions and not enough answers. Some things my eyes were soon opened to:

a. There is much more to discover than our human nature is tuned in to.

b. There are pits of mental and emotional quicksand that will gradually swallow us up with careless or misguided steps.

c. If we continue to walk in the darkness of spirit that we are borne into, we could easily step off the edge of a cliff to be awakened by the misery at the bottom and by each glancing impact on the way down.

d. We can spend the duration of our existence without taking the journey if we don't know there is one.

e. We don't have to be victims of the predators that can attack us from within.

f. Our spirit waits for the touch of life and renewal that allows us to discover who we really are and the treasures that are hidden within.

g. Our true worth is not determined from without, but from within.

h. *"It is the spirit who gives life; the flesh provides no benefit; the words that I have spoken to you are spirit and are life."* (John 6:63) (Focusing on, and receiving, the correctly spoken "Word" is powerful enough to change your life.)

i. The human nature we are born with is tuned in to the temporary things of this world that are always changing, and it is constantly influenced by things beyond our awareness.

j. We all have a divine nature that awaits our acceptance and will give a new perspective; of life, purpose, and peace; that can't be found anywhere else.

Questions to Ponder:

1. What would you give to discover your personal worth to God?

2. How could a value be calculated, to apply to the worth, of someone thinking you are worth dying for? (Your value is immeasurable!)

Learning of the Needed Foundation

Shortly after I experienced the cleaning of that dreadful hopelessness which had taken over my thoughts and emotions, I felt it was continuing to lurk on the threshold of my mind, ready to jump back in. The effect my selfish human nature had on distorting and mismanaging my thoughts and emotions was still ingrained in me. I didn't understand at that time that I had been given a new divine nature that needed to be nurtured and strengthened by a relationship with the Holy Spirit.

I began studying the Bible with a passion for the truth of life that would keep the hopeless misery, I had known before, from finding its way in again. I knew, time in prayer and study would open the way for God's guidance.

I wanted the standards that were unshakeable and enriching to guide me each day. I needed a foundation to build on. I needed a guide to lead me away from the darkness that almost swallowed me up and seemed to be waiting to close in again.

One day I had a strong urge to begin writing, and I was given the verses and affirmations that I have included in "The Daily Walk" section of this book. It seemed as though I could sense a small, loving voice, deep within, that I needed to follow, giving me these powerful thoughts. I didn't know it at the time, but I was being guided to begin the construction of an unshakable foundation.

I committed to reading and focusing on the verses and affirmations each day. I didn't rely on my own understanding of them. I spent time listening for the small, quiet, loving voice within, that gave them to me as I read each one.

They seemed more powerful than the thoughts and emotions that haunted me from the past. Each time I focused on them, they erased more and more of the power, of an old existence. They gave me a strong confidence and direction for my life, and I have never been the same.

Spirit-filled words give strength and growth to the divine nature the Holy Spirit brings to life in us through our belief in Jesus Christ. My spirit, had been given life and had a strong appetite for God's Word.

- *"For the word of God is living and active, and sharper than any two-edged sword, even penetrating as far as the division of soul and spirit, of both joints and*

marrow, and able to judge the thoughts and intentions of the heart." Hebrews 4:12

If you ever have an intruding thought or emotion taking you in a direction you don't want to go, just focus on God's Word, and witness your freedom!

Now I know hopelessness and despair have no power to re-enter unless I accept them and allow their return. I found that the loving gift of scripture verses and affirmations that I was inspired to write down, were life enriching and filled with new insights that arose each time I read over them. They gradually erased the power of old thoughts and emotions that had bound and tormented me for most of my life. A verse I came to understand, with an unwavering gratitude, is:

- "*Therefore, if anyone is in Christ, this person is a new creation; the old things passed away; behold, new things have come.*" 2 Corinthians 5:17.

This is not a journey that can be seen or understood before it is begun. The need to listen to the small voice that calls for your attention will be increasingly evident with each step you take under His guidance. Allow me to give an illustration of following the voice that guides to ever increasing freedom and change in the next section.

Questions to Ponder:

1. Have you ever been taught "sticks and stones will break my bones, but words will never hurt me"?

2. Can you remember a time when you were either encouraged or discouraged by what you were told?

- *"Death and life are in the power of the tongue, and those who love it will eat its fruit."* Proverbs 18:21

Listening For Guidance

My wife, daughter, son, and I took a trip to Kentucky, from North Dakota, when our son and daughter were about seven and nine years of age. After we arrived there, I was caught up completely, all afternoon for the first day, visiting with family trying to catch up, after several years of being away. The day slipped by very quickly and I became nervously aware that I hadn't seen or heard from our son Michael for the entire afternoon. Adding to my uneasiness was the fact that it was beginning to get dark.

There was a thick forest beginning about 25 yards behind my parent's house which drew my attention quickly, because I knew my son's adventurous nature. I knew I had very little time to find him before it would get completely dark. I went up a small hill where my voice would carry as far as possible. I shaped my hands like a bull horn and gave the loudest yell of his name I could muster toward the forest.

After the second yell, a strong feeling of fear had begun to sweep ever me. I listened with a fearful strain. I heard a very tiny voice, barely finding its way through the trees to my searching ears. Sensing he was probably lost, I yelled every few seconds, so he could follow my voice. Sure enough, a very scared little boy emerged from the forest right in front of me after about fifteen minutes.

I felt like celebrating. He then entered a warm home, where he was welcomed and wrapped with the feeling of safety and security. The fear of uncertainty and danger that the approaching darkness of night brought was soon erased and rendered powerless by Michael listening and following my voice out of that darkening forest.

Question to Ponder:

1. Does any ego have good listening skills?

2. Do you have to want to listen before you can hear?

- *"I will ask the Father, and He will give you another Helper, so that He may be with you forever; the helper is the Spirit of truth, whom the world cannot receive, because it does not see Him or know Him; but you know Him because He remains with you and will be in you."* John 14:16-17

Never Out of Reach

No matter how embedded you may be in any undesirable intruding thoughts and emotions, the still, quiet, loving voice of the Holy Spirit can reach you. When you place a positive, life enriching thought of God's Word in your mind and rest in it, it not only frees your mind, it guides your heart. He will guide you in a better direction. Identifying and recognizing the thoughts and emotions that are damaging and disrupting to your wellbeing enables you to erase their power over you, with the correct counter thoughts. The powerful, yet simple, thoughts that are laid out in this journey, particularly in "The Daily Walk," are carefully chosen because of their ability to erase the potency of unwanted, destructive, thought and emotional intruders. Following the journey laid out in this book, from the beginning, will lead to an all-important, daily walk, that includes the valuable truths, that are explained along the way.

Regardless of where you stand emotionally, mentally, or spiritually at the present time, that is where you can begin this journey. Your acceptance of the "Invitation," as given to you personally, will begin your journey of a lifetime and prepare you for the daily walk. Your personal invitation is waiting for your acceptance as written in the upcoming chapter of this book. Remember, you will not be taking this journey alone. Acceptance of the

"Invitation" that is written in the next chapter will begin an eternal friendship.

- *"Behold I stand at the door and knock; if anyone hears My voice and opens the door, I will come in to him and will dine with him, and he with Me."* Revelation 3:20

Questions to Ponder:

1. Have you ever experienced a negative thought grabbing you like a Pitbull and dragging you toward the dark shadows of emotional misery?

- *"Therefore, humble yourselves under the mighty hand of God, so that He may exalt you at the proper time, having cast your anxiety on Him, because He cares about you. Be of sober spirit, be on the alert. Your adversary, the devil, prowls around like a roaring lion, seeking someone to devour. So, resist him, firm in your faith, knowing that the same experiences of suffering are being accomplished by your brothers and sisters who are in the world. After you have suffered for a little while, the God of all grace, who called you to His eternal glory in Christ will Himself perfect, confirm, strengthen, and establish you."* 1 Peter 5:6-9

(When God builds your foundation through your faith in Jesus Christ by your humble, loving obedience in all your trials and your resistance to the evil one, you cannot have a more secure foundation.)

2. How did you get freedom, or are you still trying to get free?

- *"The steadfast of mind you will keep in perfect peace, because he trusts in you. Trust in the Lord forever, for in God the Lord, we have an everlasting Rock."* Isaiah 26:3-4

(Don't just passively allow your thoughts to go where they may one more second! After understanding and accepting the "Invitation", Reflect on the thoughts in "The Daily Walk" throughout each day and gain true freedom in the Lord.)

Preparation For the Invitation

Having the right thoughts to set a good foundation is one thing, but gaining the true understanding and wisdom of those thoughts to ensure proper construction is another. Learning to listen to the quiet voice within, through the divine nature of Christ, when accepted, connects us to our guide that will show us the way of victory and authority in Christ. Not listening to that small, quiet voice of the guiding Holy Spirit will leave our interpretation of the correct thoughts up to ourselves, which is like putting tools in the hands of a newborn and expecting progress.

Our Divine nature will free our mind and emotions from the effects of the old sinful human nature but it will take focus and commitment. When we accept the gift of divine nature in Jesus Christ, we also receive the gift of guidance, teaching, wisdom, and understanding of the truth through the person of the Holy Spirit. There is more to be understood about our gift of God's grace concerning the divine nature of Jesus Christ and the guidance of the Holy Spirit. The deeper wisdom and understanding come, as "The Daily Walk" takes you further on this journey of "Discovery, Freedom, and Life".

We have made our own decisions according to the values and standards we have developed, according to our adjustments and lessons learned, through our human nature, to make life bearable or enjoyable as best we could. It is easy to think or feel like we have no choice in the quality of our life at times. When we learn, we have the ability to choose and manage what we think and feel, with the guidance of the Holy Spirit of God through Christ, we no longer get forced in different directions by random influences. Our life can change completely, under the authority of Jesus Name and God's Word.

- *"Watch over your heart with all diligence for from it flow the springs of life."* Proverbs 4:23

Our heart (spirit) occupies its place of neglect and subordination, even servanthood, in its relationship to our fleshly desires, or thought and emotional free-for-all, until we learn what to do about it.

Questions to Ponder:

1. What would you say to God if you knew He was listening?

2. Do you know Him well enough to speak that way?

See What's Missing

Our true ability to manage our thoughts and emotions was designed to come from the divine nature that God originally gave to the father and mother of all people, Adam and Eve. When they lost that divine nature (connection to God) through disobedience and selfishness, they were left with the empty, short sighted, self-indulgent, self-defeating, sinful human nature that guides all of us now from the time we are born until we learn what to do about it.

Human nature is vulnerable to the deception of things our senses are not tuned in to. Our heart (spirit) gets cluttered and distorted with deceptive, self-defeating direction from our vulnerable human nature which is influenced one way or the other by things we cannot see as well as the ones we can see.

We cannot be enriched and guided by the divine nature until we receive it through a renewed relationship with God. Through God's loving grace and forgiveness, we are all offered the great gift of that divine nature in Jesus Christ. Through the ability the divine nature of Christ gives to listen to the Holy Spirit's quiet, loving voice within, we gain understanding and wisdom that shapes our unshakable foundation.

Trying to clean and manage our thought and emotional condition strictly under the authority and guidance of our vulnerable human nature is comparable to having all doors open in the middle of a dust storm while trying to clean house.

Questions to Ponder:

1. Have you ever felt an emptiness inside?

2. What have you tried to fill that emptiness with?

Poised For Listening

All of us need to listen for the loving, compassionate voice that makes its way amidst all the pain and distractions of our lives. Most of us don't seem to pay attention to that voice until the dreaded darkness of this world seems to be about to swallow us up. Many times, that voice comes to us through someone we have never seen before.

Friend, consider the words on these pages as an introduction to the voice that can guide you out of the thoughts and emotions that may be casting a dark shadow over your life.

The journey that leads from the weakening, struggling, blind and vulnerable effects of the old sinful human nature, to a thriving divine nature, is of utmost importance:

- Jesus said, "*I came so that they would have life, and have it abundantly.*" John 10:10

It's a journey that cannot be taken without the proper guide. It is the growing relationship with the guide that enables us to take the next step each day. Listening to the quiet inner voice of the Holy Spirit (guide) enables our new divine nature's ability to see our new freedom, wisdom, and understanding, as we need it. Humble obedience to that quiet, loving voice speaking to our heart, leads to the replacement of an unsteady foundation with an unshakable foundation for our mental and emotional home.

Questions to Ponder:

1. Have you ever been totally ignored by the very person you could easily help avoid trouble?

2. How do you think the Holy Spirit feels when our selfish desires drown out His voice?

Introduction to a Divine Friendship

After much prayer and study of the Bible, I began to learn more about a person than a ticket (the idea of a person). I discovered within its pages a magnificent, loving letter of invitation. It's an invitation to personally walk with God in a way we may have thought out of our reach.

I have compiled what I have seen throughout the Bible as that loving letter of invitation into a shorter version that I believe is the invitation to all of us. When this invitation is understood and accepted, an inner spiritual door is opened. This door gives entrance to the person who brings endless possibilities of life.

- Jesus said, *"Behold I stand at the door, and knock: if anyone hears My voice and opens the door, I will come in to him and will dine with him, and he with Me."* Revelation 3:20

Your acquaintance with God in Jesus Christ, will grow with sincere desire, humble focus and discipline, living as He guides you, and prayer. He offers, unconditional love, forgiveness, peace, joy, freedom, wisdom, and truth, in His righteousness. These treasures of life grow as you come to know Him more and more.

- *"Grace and peace be multiplied unto you in the knowledge of God and of Jesus our Lord."* 2 Peter 1:2

These gifts can begin to quickly fade, if the distractions of life capture your attention more than He does. Focusing on your walk with God each day can bring the inspiration of heart (spirit) that erodes the power of distorted adjustments of past thoughts and emotions. His guidance also enables the management of all thoughts and emotions going forward.

This isn't an accomplishment or an arrival for you. It is the beginning of a journey. A journey you walk each day with Him as He teaches you to discover how to be full of His life, in a world that is painfully empty.

Questions to Ponder:

1. Do you think the invitation in the next chapter, really pertains to you?

- *"For all have sinned and fall short of the glory of God, being justified as a gift by His grace through the redemption which is in Christ Jesus, whom God displayed publicly as a propitiation in His blood through faith."* Romans 3:23-25

2. What impact do you think this invitation could have on your life, now and forever?

- *"For the wages of sin is death, but the gracious gift of God is eternal life in Christ Jesus our Lord."* Romans 6:23

- *"Therefore, if anyone is in Christ, this person is a new creation; the old things passed away; behold, new things have come."* 2 Corinthians 5:17

(To clarify, to believe in Christ and repent of your sins is to receive the divine nature of Christ and the guidance of the Holy Spirit, and the opportunity to walk with God each day.)

Finally, a Place to Start

Before that day of renewal, my spirit was smothered, broken, and lifeless. That day, it was mended and given the ability to hear the still, small, loving voice that would direct me out of the deep darkness that nearly swallowed me completely. A divine relationship began that I barely understood.

The hand that took hold of my ankle that day is the same hand that is reaching out to you. You may not be in such an extreme situation as I was. You may not be in an emotionally or mentally painful situation at all. The truth is that unconditional love, peace that surpasses understanding, and strength to overcome all the difficulties of life, are all offered to everyone as gifts in a renewed relationship with God through Jesus Christ.

Being in the condition to receive the gifts and hold on to them is of utmost importance to understand. My desire is to walk with you on this journey of the mind, emotions, and the heart by giving "The Daily Walk" to you as it was given to me, to help build your understanding.

Unlike the mental and emotional intruders that come to live in our house through unmanaged adjustments, the gifts wait to be accepted from someone we all have the opportunity to know.

- *" For, God so loved the world, that He gave His only Son, so that everyone who believes in Him will not perish, but have eternal life."* John 3:16

God has made the relationship renewal possible. We can know *of* Jesus and not really *know* Him. It is important to be able to hear (sense) the knock at the door of our spirit (heart) when He knocks.

- *"Behold I stand at the door and knock; if anyone hears My voice and opens the door, I will come in to him, and will dine with him, and he with Me."* Revelation 3:20

Simply hearing the truth, of how God has made it possible for all of us to know Him through Jesus Christ, is a knock at your door. Belief and acceptance of the truth in "The Invitation" chapter of this book will open your spiritual door.

These following words describe a personal, ongoing relationship, more like a sustained friendship. Only you can open that door. An attitude of humility will prepare your heart for this sacred friendship (knowing you have need of the love, grace, and forgiveness given in Jesus Christ). Know a great price was paid, preparing for your acceptance (know God accepts you into His family of believers). An attitude of gratitude is important for the eternal relationship you are being offered (truly be thankful for Christ's payment of the penalty for you). Be open to a true sense of awe (it is through Jesus Christ you have access to God).

The Holy Spirit can enable a heart conditioned in such a way to faithfully receive the one who embodies the life of God, through belief and repentance. Belief, is accepting what Jesus has done for you, and repentance is turning to God's ways for your life.

Unconditional love and acceptance; a renewed divine relationship of spirit with God through Christ; an awakening to new knowledge and understanding; these are just the beginning of your new walk with God through faith in Christ. Sounds like a lot to take in, doesn't it?

To avoid any hesitation or confusion, "The Daily Walk" chapter is designed to guide anyone, from the first moment of belief or after many years of belief, in a mental, emotional, and heart journey of discovery, freedom, and life. The journey's map, of "The Daily Walk", was given to me forty-two years ago. I follow it today. Open your heart now and receive the invitation of a lifetime which will position you to begin your walk with God, which just gets more enlightening and strengthening every day. Throughout God's Word is revealed, the invitation for all of us, to see our need to walk with Him, and begin an eternal, victorious relationship. Read the invitation as a personal letter to you, from God.

Questions to Ponder:

1. What is the most valuable gift you have ever been given?

2. Were you exited enough to talk about it?

Section Three:

Life

Chapter Five:

Invitation

Need of Renewal

Dear (Your name),

I formed the father and mother of mankind to walk with Me eternally. We had a loving relationship through the divine nature I gave them. There was a fall from my grace a long time ago by them through unbelief, disobedience, and selfishness. They were deceived by the father of all lies.

He and his helpers seek to blind and mislead all who need to come back to walking with me today. His name is Satan. He cunningly deceived Adam and Eve into surrendering the dominion I gave to them. When they accepted and followed his deceptive direction, they gave their authority to him. That meant he had dominion over humankind from that point. He and his helpers have wreaked havoc in the lives of people from that day till now.

Their goal is the eternal death of the hearts and souls of all people. I limited their power to immediately destroy people, because My love, compassion, and forgiveness were not diminished by the disobedience of Adam and Eve. I will explain how my hand of grace is extended to all people, especially you. When they were filled with My divine nature, they knew their purpose and significance, and they knew their position with me. They knew they were created by Me and were to live in My spirit of life. My divine nature within them enabled our personal relationship.

Separated from Me through their disobedience, they gave up the divine nature which enabled our relationship. They lost their purpose and received the curse of physical and spiritual death with the sin nature they surrendered to at that time. All people have been borne under that same separation and curse, from that day, through that sin nature.

- *"For all have sinned and fall short of the glory of God."* Romans 3:23

Without My spirit there is no spiritual life. The nature that filled and determined the daily existence of mankind from that time till now has been that same sinful (separated from Me) human nature.

The love is unconditional, that brought My Son to be born into this world to die in your place, to pay the penalty of death, for you. That means you are offered My gift of divine love, forgiveness and eternal life, without a cost to you; He has paid the cost in full.

- *"For the wages of sin is death; but the gracious gift of God is eternal life in Christ Jesus our Lord."* Romans 6:23

When He paid the penalty of death for you, He also gave the dominion back to you, which makes Satan and his helpers powerless over you. Unfortunately, many believers know very little about the authority they have been given, through their faith in Jesus My Son.

The only power and authority Satan and his helpers have over you is what you allow them to have! Too many believers struggle under that false authority, because they don't understand the divine authority, I have given back to them.

- *"Because greater is He who is in you, than he who is in the world"* 1 John 4:4

The divine nature of Jesus My Son in you, gives you authority. It is because of what Jesus accomplished in His life — torture and death on the cross, resurrection from the dead, and ascension — that His divine authority is given to you through belief, repentance, and loving, humble obedience. That is why our walk together is so important. I will help you understand the freedom, authority, and victory you can have in every encounter you have with the deceiver.

Questions to Ponder

1. Should you be afraid at any time in your "Daily Walk"?

*   *"For God has not given us a spirit of timidity, but of power and love and discipline."* 2 Timothy 1:7

(When fear tries to take hold of you in anything, go to God in prayer and search His word, while listening for the quiet, loving guidance of His Holy Spirit.)

*   *"Peace, I leave with you, My peace I give to you; not as the world gives, do I give to you. Do not let your hearts be troubled, nor fearful."* John 14:27

(Jesus is the "Prince of Peace." Just look to Him for a heart adjustment.)

2. What can you do to always be the overcomer?

*   *"Finally, be strong in the Lord and in the strength of His might. Put on the full armor of God, so that you will be able to stand firm against the schemes of the devil."* Ephesians 6:10-11

(Putting on the full armor of God each day is a conscious choice in the development of a lifestyle of humble, loving obedience and learning the power in His Word and the name of Jesus, as "The Daily Walk" guides you in doing.)

Personal and Eternal

I'm so glad you are reading my letter. This message is meant especially for you. I've tried so long to get your attention. I have linked life in this world with time. Everyone has their allotted time for life. You and I can walk together as I show you what I have for you. Many settle for just knowing of me, and continue their walk alone. They don't realize how vulnerable they are without Me. The present moment of time is when you and I can create and begin a walk of discovery, triumph, freedom, and endless possibilities.

It's very easy for you to get caught up in the temporary, meaningless distractions that always leave you empty and disappointed in the end. That is the nature of the world; to offer you false hopes and make you think you can fulfill your needs with material things. There is nothing in the world that can replace the gifts I have for you.

You were born into a physical, mental, emotional, and spiritual life that has been under the authority of sinful human nature. That sinful human nature has been under the authority of the great deceiver, who is committed to your present and eternal destruction (Satan and his helpers). They rebelled against Me long ago and were cast out of heaven. They have an eternal destination where they will be sent on the "Day of Judgment". Their hatred for Me drives them to destroy as much of My creation as possible, especially the crown of My creation, which is mankind.

I want you to know I have stripped them of any authority over you, through the victory of My Son Jesus Christ over them. His victory is applied to you, as if you personally accomplished the same thing, when you lovingly, gratefully, humbly, believe and receive Him as Lord and savior of your life now and forever. However, they will continue to exercise false authority over your thoughts and emotions if you don't know how to resist them. I have given you authority over them through Jesus Christ My Son.

I want to restore the relationship between you and Me that was lost long ago, before you were born. I want to give you the gifts you would have had if there had been no loss of relationship between us. The thoughts and emotions that have guided or misguided you up to now, were influenced by the circumstances and people or things of this world.

You were created to be influenced physically, spiritually, mentally, and emotionally for your ultimate good, through your relationship with Me. It is My will that our relationship be renewed through your faith in My gift of unconditional love and forgiveness in My Son Jesus Christ. The determining factor in your life from this point on is whether you believe in Me and My gift.

- *"These things I have written to you who believe in the name of the Son of God, so that you may know that you have eternal life."* 1 John 5:13

When you believe, your life begins. It isn't something reserved for a future time; it begins now!

Questions to Ponder:

1. Does your position or importance in the world make any difference in when, where, why, or how you start your walk with God?

- *"As many as received Him, to them He gave the right to become children of God, to those who believe in His name."* John 1:12

2. How important is your attitude toward God's ways?

- *"The time is fulfilled, and the kingdom of God has come near; repent and believe the gospel"* Mark 1:15

(Repenting is turning from the ways of selfish human nature, to follow the ways of God through the divine nature given to you through belief in Jesus Christ.)

True Fulfillment

The proper thoughts carry a lasting influence. The principal thoughts for you are truth and grace. The truth is, I created you in my image. That means you have a spiritual void that exists because of the break in our relationship. This void cannot be cured or fulfilled by anything in this physical world. You have a natural drive to fill that void in the depths of your being:

1. You need to be loved completely and unconditionally and be able to extend that same love, from within, in a relationship with Me and others.
2. You need to discover who you really are and who you were meant to be.
3. You need to have a sense of belonging and meaning that never fades but gets stronger each day.
4. You need to be free from the fear that is inherent in everyone but might not be clearly understood; Fear of eternal, spiritual death; That is separation from Me for eternity, which leaves you vulnerable to the torments of darkness now and eternally.

5. You need My peace and wisdom that will guide you while navigating through this merciless world, for your good and for others.

I have the answers to all these needs and I long to give them to everyone, especially you. My unconditional gift of grace to you through faith in Jesus My Son will position you to begin our walk together.

- *"For by grace you have been saved through faith; and this is not a result of works, so that no one may boast. For we are His workmanship, created in Christ Jesus for good works, which God prepared beforehand so that we would walk in them,"* Ephesians 2:8-10

I have given my Word of life, in the Holy Scriptures, by My apostles and prophets. Open your heart to My word, and I will show you, My ways. I must say, walking with the impersonal idea of Me, while fulfilling common rituals recognized as good spiritual responsibilities, is not necessarily walking with Me.

- *"Jesus answered and said to him, "if anyone loves Me, He will follow My word; and My Father will love him, and We will come to him and make our dwelling with him."* John 14:23

Prayerful, loving, humble obedience will build our relationship by removing the obstacles that may try to separate us. I have brought you to read this letter because it is your time to receive what I have for you. I don't require any special qualification or condition of perfection for you to receive these things. I have many gifts for you. All gifts are given through belief in My Son Jesus Christ as you walk with Me each day.

However, there are certain mental attitudes that your circumstances may have caused you to adopt which will prevent you from seeing and receiving what I have ready for you. Some of these attitudes are pride, selfishness, jealousy, fear, doubt, anger, hatred, lust, greed, resentment, and many other negative mental attitudes.

These things are all binding, blinding, and life draining. They are all the workings of a selfish human nature that is separated from Me. Don't let yourself be a victim of any of these for any length of time. I can help you with them if you allow Me.

- *"And looking at them, Jesus said to them, "with people this is impossible, but with God all things are possible"* Mathew 19:26

The words of Jesus are meant to give you victory and life.

Questions to Ponder

1. Do you think the thoughts entering your mind right now are your own or are they coming from some other source?

• *"For the weapons of our warfare are not of the flesh, but divinely powerful for the destruction of fortresses. We are destroying arguments and all arrogance raised against the knowledge of God, and we are taking every thought captive to the obedience of Christ."* 2 Corinthians 10:4-5

(Have no doubts, your mind is the battleground where you will fall or where you stand! "The Daily Walk" will help you learn firsthand about the armor of God and the steps of adding to your faith the things that reveal God's divine power, helping you be an overcomer each day. Just continue on this journey to understand how that can happen.)

2. How important is your decision right now?

• *"Watch over your heart with all diligence, for from it flow the springs of life."* Proverbs 4:23

(You are the keeper of your heart! It requires diligence. Do not take it lightly. You are given a responsibility of maintaining an open path for life, as God chose through Jesus Christ, to establish the example and the means for life to flow through one, to many.)

Free to Choose

I ask you to free yourself of any biases or prejudices and any blinding negative thoughts at this time. If you ask Me, I can help you through the authority I have placed in my Son's name, "Jesus." Just humbly and respectfully thinking on His name brings My loving attention to you. I am as close as your own thoughts. I have given you the ability to exercise your free will. Let these next few minutes be a special time between you and Me.

I do know your thoughts, and I do know what you hold in your heart as the guidelines for your life. Truly believe what I am revealing to you now. Your belief will begin your relationship with My Son, who will give you access to Me.

- *"Jesus said to him, I am the way, and the truth, and the life: no one comes to the Father except through Me"* John 14:6

He will flood your heart and mind with my unconditional love and acceptance and give you the renewal of divine nature through His spirit that will change your life through obedience, grace, and truth as you continue on this journey.

Are you ready to receive what I have waited to give especially you? I have set before you a journey. It is a journey that has indescribable spiritual riches along the way. It is one designed especially for you.

This just remains an invitation to you delivered through the words in this book until you begin to believe. Up to now you may have disciplined your mind in any number of ways to grow and mature and expand your capabilities, looking for the rewards of self-accomplishment. You may have allowed your mind to wonder freely across any interesting field of thought that came along hoping to grasp some passing sense of meaning or relief.

I want to flood your very being with new life, unconditional love and a complete forgiveness so that you and I may begin an eternal relationship. These are among the gifts I have for you that will enable you to walk with Me each day. So many misunderstand the reason for these gifts. They think they receive My loving deliverance from an eternal torment just to have passage into a future destination called heaven with no real concern for the journey. They just settle to remain bound by the adjustments and false authority of their old sinful human nature.

- *"So, Jesus was saying to those Jews who had believed Him, "If you continue in My word, then you are*

> *truly My disciples; and you will know the truth, and the truth will set you free."* John 8:31-32

Let the Word of My truth be established in your mind and heart. The seed of my truth will grow to fill your heart with my grace that will shine to show you the treasures along this daily journey.

Questions to Ponder

1. Can you truly walk with God, while ignoring any acknowledgement of His presence, until it is in your best interest?

- *"If you remain in Me, and My words remain you, ask whatever you wish, and it will be done for you. My Father is glorified by this, that you bear much fruit, and so prove to be My disciples."* John 15:7-8

(Building a relationship requires an ever-enriching familiarity through the Holy Spirit by doing all things for the glory of God in humble, loving obedience.)

2. What should you do if deceptive influences attempt to lead you to think walking with God is burdensome?

- "*Come to Me, all who are weary and burdened, and I will give you rest. Take My yoke upon you and learn from Me, for I am gentle and humble in heart, and you will find rest for your souls. For My yoke is comfortable, and My burden is light.*" Matthew 11:28-30

(When walking with God becomes burdensome, it only means you need to get your mind off yourself, and get your mind on Christ.)

The Unconditional Gift

You cannot earn it. You cannot precondition yourself in any fashion to be worthy to receive it. I will give you My unconditional love and forgiveness, as a gift, through your faith, in what My only begotten Son, Jesus Christ, has done for you in obedience to Me. I don't expect you to understand all this right now. I will help you see My truth as we take this journey together.

- "*For the Lord gives wisdom; from His mouth come knowledge and understanding.*" Proverbs 2:6

So far, you may have been wondering why you are alive, or what is your purpose? Let me show you the answers to these questions and many more. Your thoughts and emotions are vulnerable without My daily influence through your new divine nature in taking authority over old deceptive influences. I will guide you back to living in that divine nature, which was lost.

The fall from grace left a price of death to pay for all of mankind, because without me, there is no life. Even though you physically live and breathe for a time, you do not have the eternal spirit of life in you that I offer you now through faith in Jesus My Son. Your relationship with Him gives you access to Me.

The spirit that has been residing as part of you up to this time has had no connection with my spirit of life. That is why the feelings of pride, selfishness, emptiness, loneliness, fear, insignificance, and the deep need to belong have led you on a desperate search for answers and may continue to drive you in so many different ways.

You and I know that physical death simply allows the body to go back to the earth. The spiritual death is far from the same thing. I have given each member of mankind a spirit. That spirit, begins, hidden behind and beneath all the desires of the flesh and the pride of life, because of the fall from My grace. The spirit of each person has no life in it until a relationship with Me is renewed through faith in Jesus Christ. It is that part of you that you may feel moaning and groaning at times because it has no life and it is totally at the mercy of the flesh, the world, and all the forces that reside therein.

Questions to Ponder

1. Is it possible to live your whole life without knowing your spiritual poverty?

- *"People having been filled with all unrighteousness, wickedness, greed, and evil; full of envy, murder, strife, deceit, and malice; they are gossips, slanderers, haters of God, insolent, arrogant, boastful, inventors of evil, disobedient to parents, without understanding, untrustworthy, unfeeling, and unmerciful; and although they know the ordinance of God, that those who practice such things are worthy of death, they not only do the same, but also approve of those who practice them,"* Romans 1:29-32

(Many are deceived and blind to their need. But many are aware of their spiritual poverty and don't care; the authority of their sinful human nature has been given too much power. If you are reading this invitation, it isn't by accident. You have been given the ability to choose God's grace and truth or remain in spiritual poverty.)

2. Can a person who is in spiritual poverty have a solid foundation for life?

- *"Like a city that is broken into and without walls so is a person who has no self-control over his spirit."* Proverbs 25:28

(Spiritual poverty makes people vulnerable to the false authority and deception of the old, sinful human nature and the dark influences that exercise authority over it.)

What You Can't See Can Hurt

You may have wondered at times why you do certain things when you really don't want to do them. With the passage of time and gradual surrendering to the desires of the flesh and the world around you, your self-governing authority fades and puts you at the mercy of any rogue thought or emotion like a slave under the control of a master.

Satan and his helpers have tremendous influence over your thoughts and emotions. They are very good at making you think they are your own thoughts and emotions. That is their area of expertise; lies and deception, with your destruction in mind. That lifeless spiritual condition is what I want to change for you and all who will believe.

Many who begin to believe don't know the next step to take so they spend each day wrestling with thoughts and emotions that seem to pull them in the old direction.

Your thoughts and emotions are directly linked to your relationship with me.

- *"The steadfast of mind You will keep in perfect peace, because he trusts in you."* Isaiah 26: 3-4

The truth and grace I can reveal to you through a humble, loving walk with Me, allows Me to give you the gifts, that will enable you to have an unshakable foundation to build your life on, no matter how unworthy you think you are.

I took the question of your worthiness out of the picture by offering My unconditional love and forgiveness through My Son Jesus' sacrifice of His own life for you. If you never choose to believe in what I reveal to you now, your spirit will pass from your body at the time of your physical death and go to a place where all spirits will go that are not under my grace, awaiting the day of judgement for eternity.

That place will be occupied with the forces of darkness which work to blind you from the truth of my love and forgiveness in this world. They will be dedicated to making your spiritual, eternal existence, an agonizing, eternal hell. They are already destined for eternal torment. They just want to take as many unsuspecting lost souls with them as they can. I don't want you to go there. And you don't have to.

81

It is not my desire to scare you into mistakenly thinking you can escape torment by getting your free ticket to heaven. It is my deepest desire to restore you to a loving walk with Me now and eternally. Believing in Jesus My Son; confessing He is your Savior and Lord because of what he has done for you; and humble obedience begins your walk with Me.

He has prepared an eternal home for you and all those who believe and confess. I cannot allow unbelievers or any powers of darkness to be there. They will be in their own place which is reserved for them for eternity.

Please receive My unconditional love and forgiveness this day. Let the emptiness you have had be replaced with a fullness only I can give. It is My sincere desire to restore your relationship with Me now, to avoid any further separation and emptiness. I desire to walk with you daily and show you your true life now and for eternity.

Questions to Ponder

1. Why did Jesus Christ, the Son of God, appear in this world?

- *"The Son of God appeared for this purpose, to destroy the works of the devil."* 1 John 3:8

(Because Jesus Christ came to represent mankind before God, everything He accomplished — living a sinless life, paying the penalty of your sin by dying on the cross, rising from death and the grave, ascending to the right hand of the throne of grace — is applied eternally to you through your belief and confession in what He has done. Repentance and loving, humble obedience bring the victory forward in your life.)

2.   Do you know the things Jesus came to undo?

- *"The Spirit of the Lord God is upon me, because the Lord anointed me to bring good news to the humble; He has sent me to bind up the broken hearted, to proclaim release to the captives and freedom to prisoners; To proclaim the favorable year of the Lord and the day of vengeance of our God; To comfort all who mourn, to grant those who mourn in Zion, giving them a garland instead of ashes, the oil of gladness instead of mourning, the cloak of praise instead of a disheartened spirit. So, they will be called oaks of righteousness, the planting of the Lord, that He may be glorified."* Isaiah 61:1-3

(God has made it possible for you to be free of the dominion of Satan and no longer to live in spiritual poverty. It is through faith in Jesus Christ, so many things are undone, and so many things are possible, walking with God in Christ.)

Love And Grace Extended to You

I displayed to the world my full acceptance of my Son's sacrifice when He died on the cross for every person's sin and separation from Me, by raising Him from the dead three days after His crucifixion and burial.

- *"But He was pierced because of our transgressions, crushed because of our iniquities; punishment for our peace was on Him. And we are healed by His wounds. We all went astray like sheep: we all have turned to our own way: and the Lord has punished Him for the iniquity of us all."* Isaiah 53:5-6

He waits to live in your heart and fill you with His divine nature which gives you the victory and freedom from the powers of the flesh, the world, and the forces of darkness, through your humble, loving obedience. These are the things He defeated through His death and resurrection. He then ascended to the right hand of My throne of grace as the Lord of all. When He lives in your heart through belief, confession, and repentance, you have access to My throne through Him because My same complete acceptance, of His sacrifice and victory, is extended to you.

This condition of renewed divine nature within you, begins the spiritual eternal life in you, which means your purpose and significance are renewed with Me eternally. I wait to begin this journey of freedom and life with you.

It isn't a journey I force on you. It is a journey for you to get to know me better each day.

- *"But the path of the righteous is like the light of dawn that shines brighter and brighter until the full day."* Proverbs 4:18

That full day is when you will be received in the special place My Son Jesus has prepared for you. Jesus said,

- *"In My Father's house are many rooms; if that were not so, I would have told you, because I am going there to prepare a place for you. And if I go and prepare a place for you, I am coming again, and will take you to Myself, so that where I am, there you also will be."* John 14:2-3

My Son Jesus Christ rose from the dead on the third day, by the power of the Holy Spirit, to ascend and be seated on the right hand of my throne of grace. At that time, I sent My Holy Spirit to inspire, teach, comfort, and guide all believers on their journey of learning to walk each day in My will under the authority of Jesus' name.

I, (your Father), Jesus (My Son, your savior), and the Holy Spirit, are all of one spirit working for you and within you, for your life now, and eternally, to be what it was meant to be. Jesus said,

- *"I came so that they would have life and have it abundantly."* John 10:10

You don't have to understand all this to begin this walk of freedom and life. Let us begin this blessed eternal journey together. Jesus represents you and your interests before Me, with perfect love and compassion and wisdom. Through faith in Him, the Holy Spirit will form His mind and strengthen His divine nature in you as you walk this journey of faith. Your belief and repentance (turning from your human nature desires to divine nature desires) will begin our journey together.

My Son Jesus came to live as a man in the most humble, dreadful conditions of life so He could relate to all people, regardless of their position in life. I sent My Son as My purest, most complete expression of unconditional love for you. Will you receive My eternal, unconditional love and forgiveness now by receiving His divine nature within you? Let us walk together. Will you believe, confess Jesus Christ, My only begotten Son, as your Lord and Savior, and repent of your sins now, which means, turning from your ways to follow My ways?

With all My love through Jesus Christ My Son,

God,
Your loving Heavenly Father

Statement of Belief:

I, (your name), believe what Jesus Christ has done for me, and I turn from my way of selfish living to follow Him, living in God's will, by the guidance of the Holy Spirit who now lives in my heart. I will now humbly begin this daily journey. I will seek, through prayer and the truth, to illuminate my way walking with God in the grace given to me through the divine nature of Jesus Christ, my Lord and Savior, now within me.

Chapter Six:

Get Ready for the Walk

A Newfound Authority

This brings your spirit to its rightful place of authority over desires of the flesh, mental and emotional adjustments (past, present, and future), and enables you to break the bonds that have been created by past distorted adjustments. Having that authority and knowing how to use it are two different things.

- *"The fear of the Lord is the beginning of knowledge."* Proverbs 1:7

Learning how to listen for the guidance within is of utmost importance. Avoiding the deception of the wrong influences within, is just as important. Your new divine nature in Christ needs to grow in you through prayer, following God's word in loving obedience, listening to the small loving, guiding voice within.

Your thoughts and emotions have been conditioned toward life so far by your old sinful nature which has been under the direct influence of your spiritual enemy; Satan and his many helpers. They specialize in creating the thoughts and emotions within you that blind, tear down, destroy, deceive, confuse, bind, and keep you spiritually ineffective. Giving them authority over your life robs you of your true life. It is time to give your new divine nature the authority in your thoughts and emotions that will guide you into God's peace and life with endless potential.

When you come to a state of doubt, fear, anger, hatred, jealousy, confusion, vengeance, depression, or any other self-depreciating condition of your life, you can be assured they are at work. It is important to be able to recognize their handy work. It is just as important to know what to do about it through the divine nature of Jesus Christ and the authority you are given in His name.

Ego has no place in this new birth of divine nature authority. This authority is enabled through humble, loving obedience to the Holy Spirit that will now guide you if you listen to His small, quiet, loving voice within. Prayer and reading God's word gets you in the humble, loving, receptive state of mind and heart, where you can hear.

Being given a gift so far beyond your understanding (human understanding), may leave you unable to see where to take the next step. That can cause you to stand still spiritually. Some may even think they have their ticket to heaven, so all they have to do is wait on the heavenly express train to whisk them off to heaven when their time comes. I was one of those at one time.

This is not an accomplishment, or an arrival, but the beginning, of a divine relationship, for a daily journey, that has eternal treasures to be discovered along the way. That is why the map for "The Daily Walk" is so important. It has a starting point, which is where you are now, and a progression of growth in the awareness of walking with God each day, to a position of clarity, freedom, and stability where you will not stumble, as described in 2 Peter 1. (I will explain more later in this chapter.)

- *"The path of the righteous is like the light of dawn that shines brighter until the full day."* Proverbs 4:18

Your daily walk is the beginning of discovering eternal treasures, which God means for you to have.

Questions to Ponder:

1. How would it make you feel if someone gave you a treasure map that had 100% certainty of showing you where the treasures of a lifetime can be found?

- *"The kingdom of heaven is like a treasure hidden in the field, which a man found and hid again; and from joy over it he goes and sells everything that he has, and buys that field."* Matthew 13:45

(Even a treasure map is just another piece of paper, if the value of its purpose is not seen. When your eyes are opened to the treasures in Christ, you can see, there is nothing in this world, or within yourself, that can compare.)

2. How valuable are love, joy, peace, truth, wisdom, and understanding?

(Keep in mind that their value is measured by the actions that were necessary to make these treasures accessible to you.)

Having the Right Perspective for the Journey

You start out as a spiritual babe, no matter how old you are physically. The lack of spiritual guidance can cause you to slip into the direction of your own personal desire to advance in growth. Desire without proper guidance can deceive and burn you out in your own enthusiasm to grow spiritually; Putting all effort into going to church, getting involved in ministry, reading the Bible hours at a time, or going to every program you can sign up for, could leave you empty and frustrated.

These things are all good unless they are used in your own efforts to grow spiritually. In the midst of whatever you do, you must learn to position yourself to listen to the quiet, small voice of the Holy Spirit, who communicates with the divine nature of Christ which is given to you through faith.

Your own efforts, without the guidance of the Holy Spirit first, only lead to strengthening your own self-righteousness. Don't fall into the self-righteous trap. If you find yourself frustrated at anyone's lack of growth, get out of your ego, be still, and get into Christ. Pray, wait expectantly before God.

- *"He gives strength to the weary, and to the one who lacks might He increases power. Yet those who wait for the Lord will gain strength; They will mount up with wings like eagles, they will run and not get tired, they will walk and not become weary."* Isaiah 40:29-31

Let your strength come from God, for humble acts of obedience. Get still before God and listen until you have overcome the promptings of your selfishness. You will be able to hear the guidance that is received by your new divine nature in Jesus Christ from the Holy Spirit.

Questions to Ponder:

1. How would you describe, "waiting on God"?

(Your humble, loving, patient, receptive, thankful, attitude toward God in all situations, keeps you faithfully aware of the river of life when it flows through you to glorify God.)

2. Do you think God's schedule is affected more by what you want or by what's best for you?

• *"And we know that God causes all things to work together for good to those who love God, to those who are called according to His purpose."* Romans 8:28

(Many times, people fall into the selfish trap of blaming God for things that happen, rather than using the knowledge and abilities He has blessed us with to bring His power and glory into the world through us.)

Don't Just Stand Still!

First of all, take every opportunity to tell those who will respect your decision, you now believe in Jesus Christ as your Lord and Savior. You will be blessed by the strength that confession builds in your new gift of divine nature in Christ.

As an act that gives a physical testimony to what has happened in your spirit, seek to join a good church and be baptized. This will give witness to the truth that the power of the old human nature has been crucified in relation to the death of Christ and you have taken on the resurrection life of His divine nature the same as He displayed when He rose from the dead in total victory. It will also give witness that you are now part of the body of Christ (the church).

You have spent a lifetime under the dark influence of universal, sinful human nature. Sinful human nature came about as a result of disobedience and selfishness by the father and mother of mankind (Adam and Eve). It is dark, because of its separation from God's light of life. You have developed the habit of existing, functioning, and adjusting to life under the old authority of human nature. That human nature has been highly vulnerable to the deceptive strategies of the father of all lies (Satan). Don't forget about his helpers. Consider that old sinful human nature as being crucified with Christ. Believe you are a new creature in Christ.

Now, the divine nature of Jesus Christ has been borne within you through your belief, confession, and repentance. The foundation this relationship must begin with, and continue on, is love and faith. Be consciously aware of receiving His unconditional love, through faith in Jesus Christ, and cultivate a grateful, loving attitude toward Him constantly.

- *"Jesus answered and said to him, if anyone loves Me, he will follow my word: and My Father will love him, and we will come to him and make Our dwelling with him."* John 14:23

Look at His Word as the means to grow a loving, blessed relationship. Do not allow the deception of Satan or his helpers make the Word just a list of strict, burdensome, self-righteous rules. Prayer and listening are vital in growing your relationship with God through His Word.

Learning to see and identify the Holy Spirit's teaching and guidance will have a powerful and peaceful effect on your thoughts and emotions. That is done through studying the scriptures in conjunction with prayer.

- *"But the wisdom from above is first pure, then peace-loving, gentle, reasonable, full of mercy and good fruits, impartial, free of hypocrisy. And the fruit of righteousness is sown in peace by those who make peace."* James 3:17-18

What does it say about those who make peace?

- *"Blessed are the peacemakers: for they will be called sons of God."* Matthew 5:9

God's word and guidance are designed to create peace, wisdom, and understanding in the thoughts and emotions of believers to enable inspiring the same in others. That is accommodated by your following the promptings of the Holy Spirit in the light of God's word.

- *"The unfolding of your words gives light."* Proverbs 119:130

Many people are deceived by the old grip of Satan and his helpers and feel like they must qualify according to God's rules to look like a Christian to the world. That is pride trying to deceive and destroy. Keep it simple.

- *"For the whole law is fulfilled in one word, in the statement, "You shall love your neighbor as yourself." But I say, walk by the Spirit, and you will not carry out the desire of the flesh."* Galatians 5:14-16

Humbly seeking God's guidance through His Word and prayer, will place the authority of your decisions, with your new divine nature in Christ.

Questions to Ponder:

1. What should be your frame of mind for your daily walk with God?

- *"Have this attitude in yourselves which was also in Christ Jesus, who, as He already existed in the form of God, did not consider equality with God something to be grasped, but emptied Himself by taking the form of a bondservant and being born in the likeness of men. And being found in appearance*

as a man, He humbled Himself by becoming obe-
dient to the point of death: death on the cross."
Philippians 2:5-8

(A humble, loving attitude of obedience to God's will, your very highest priority above all else, will keep you on track.)

2.   Should you keep your faith to yourself?

*   *"And let's consider how to encourage one another*
    in love and good deeds, not abandoning our own
    meeting together, as is the habit of some people, but
    encouraging one another: and all the more as you
    see the day drawing near." Hebrews 10:24-25

(The day of the Lord's return draws closer by the day. When we get together to encourage each other, just our presence is a big encouragement to likeminded believers. The things you share may be exactly what someone else needs to hear. Let the Lord work in you and through you. Someone else may say exactly what you need to hear. Don't cheat yourself!)

Learn to Recognize Human Nature's Influence

Just be aware that your body, mind, and emotions can easily be dominated by the worlds dark influences because you have been under that authority until now. You haven't been freed from its presence; You have been freed from its authority. You just need to recognize when selfishness tries to take authority within you and turn from it by submitting to the divine nature that resides within you now. Remember, pride is of human nature.

- *"But He gives a greater grace, therefore it says, "God is opposed to the proud, but gives grace to the humble." Submit therefore to God. But resist the devil, and he will flee from you."* James 4:6-7

Getting into the habit of acknowledging God's guidance through the Holy Spirit in you, will enable the authority of your divine nature of Christ, in you, to override the authority of darkness and its influences on you.

- *"Trust in the Lord with all your heart, and do not lean on your own understanding. In all your ways acknowledge Him, and He will make your paths straight."* Proverbs 3:5-6

You may wonder, "how do I know when the darkness of selfishness is trying to take authority within me?" Take note of how your thoughts and emotions are pulling you.

- *"Now the deeds of the flesh are evident, which are: sexual immorality, impurity, indecent behavior,*

> *idolatry, witchcraft, hostilities, strife, jealousy, out-bursts of anger, selfish ambition, dissensions, fac-tions, envy, drunkenness, carousing, and things like these, of which I forewarn you, just as I have fore-warned you, that those who practice such things will not inherit the kingdom of God."* Galatians 5:19-21

Note the consequences of such things. The deeds of the flesh are binding, controlling, and contrary to the ways of the Spirit.

- *"But the fruit of the Spirit is love, joy, peace, patience, kindness, goodness, faithfulness, gentleness, self-con-trol; against such things there is no law. Now those who belong to Christ Jesus crucified the flesh with its passions and desires. If we live by the Spirit, let's follow the Spirit as well."* Galatians 5:22-25

The ways of the spirit create total freedom. Crucifying the ways of the flesh is simply turning from them to follow the ways of the spirit.

It is of utmost importance to know the divine nature of Christ in you does not forcefully take authority over your thoughts and emotions. You decide if you submit to your divine natures will in every circumstance, or not. It is not a one-time decision of authority. Through a humble, loving, and prayerful attitude of discipline and obedience, you can serve God, or through selfish weakness, deception, and blindness, you can be the slave of sin and deception.

- *"Therefore, sin is not to reign in your mortal body so that you obey its lusts, and do not go on presenting the parts of your body to sin as instruments of unrighteousness; but present yourselves to God as those who are alive from the dead, and your body's parts as instruments of righteousness for God. For sin shall not be master over you, for you are not under the law but under grace."* Romans 6:12-13

Being alive in the divine nature of Christ Jesus gives you the authority to present yourself to God as one who is now alive from the dead. Learning to make decisions in the new divine nature of Christ, with the guidance of the Holy Spirit is learning to live in God's grace. That divine guidance must be sought each day, for each decision, and in each step of your walk with God. That is a divine privilege you have in Christ. If it ever seems like a burdensome requirement, you can believe that sin is trying to wield its authority in pride and deception.

Pray and repent (turn from your understanding, to what the Holy Spirit shows you in God's Word). This should become a regular practice through a humble attitude of love and expectancy toward the Holy Spirit so He may keep you tuned in to His guiding Word. The delight of building this relationship just gets better and better each step of the way.

Treat the Holy Spirit like He is a person you love and respect. Refuse to take another step without acknowledging His presence with you. He will respond with divine gifts of love, peace, joy, longsuffering, gentleness, goodness, faith, meekness, and temperance. When you yield your thoughts and emotions to the authority of your new divine nature in Christ and open these gifts in your daily walk, you are truly becoming free from the authority of sin.

Before acting or speaking under the wrong authority, take time to acknowledge the new divine nature of Jesus Christ in you. Consciously and purposely, verbally or nonverbally, resist the pull of sin and submit to God, and Satan will leave you. He has no authority over you that you don't give him. He is very deceptive. He will try again to mislead you when you least expect it.

- *"But He gives a greater grace. Therefore; it says, "God is opposed to the proud, but gives grace to the humble." Submit therefore to God. But resist the devil, and he will flee from you."* James 4:6-7

If you ever feel like you're a million miles away from God, just do a pride check. Humbly and lovingly come before God with the attitude of being a living sacrifice to Him, willing to prove what is God's will in your life above all else. After prayer and searching His word, wait and listen.

Questions to Ponder:

1. What is the powerful and effective way to go against any authority of darkness?

(Using God's Word as the sword of the spirit, and prayerfully submitting to God in your decisions will give authority to your new divine nature in Christ.)

2. What is a sure sign that the darkness of this world is quietly and subtly trying to exert its authority in you?

- *"Peace, I leave you, My peace I give you; not as the world gives, do I give to you. Do not let your hearts be troubled, nor fearful."* John 14:27

(When the peace of Christ begins to fade, be aware and vigilant. Ask the Lord to cleanse your heart. Submit to God in prayer.)

Necessary Armor

God did not leave us defenseless. He has given us spiritual armor that I must tell you about to ensure a victorious journey. This spiritual armor is the ability of the divine nature of Christ in you to have authority over Satan, his helpers, all the darkness of this world, and everything that rises up against the knowledge of God. Every time you have a victory, which is simply resisting sin and submitting to God, the joy of the Lord grows stronger within you and the divine nature of Christ in you reveals the gifts of the Holy Spirit in your life. You will also come to know the freedom you have in Christ.

The exciting truth about the armor of God, is, you know without a doubt, that you cannot lose any spiritual battle while you stand strong in the Lord. Know that you are no longer, at the mercy of the powers of darkness that will attempt to make your thoughts and emotions toxic to hurt you.

- *"Finally, be strong in the Lord and in the strength of His might. Put on the full armor of God, so that you will be able to stand firm against the schemes of the devil. For our struggle is not against flesh and blood, but against the rulers, against the powers, against the world forces of this darkness, against the spiritual forces of wickedness in heavenly places."* Ephesians 6:10-12

First thing to understand is that you can stand against all the powers of darkness by the Lord's strength. The way you stand in the Lord's strength is by putting on God's full armor. His spiritual armor is given to protect you and enable you to be victorious in the battle against your true enemies which are not flesh and blood but spiritual. They will also influence other people against you, that are vulnerable. You have spiritual strength to overcome that also. Putting on the armor of God, sharpens your focus of faith in what Jesus has done for you and the authority He has given you; speaking and walking in His word of power according to His guidance. This is accomplished through prayer and humble obedience.

- *"But I say to you, love your enemies and pray for those who persecute you, so that you may prove yourselves to be sons of your Father who is in heaven; for He causes His sun to rise on the evil and the good, and sends rain on the righteous and the unrighteous. For if you love those who love you, what reward do you have?"* Matthew 5:44-46

The victory needed to influence people is to overcome the darkness that is influencing them, not be influenced or overcome by that same darkness. Be assured that God does not leave you or forsake you.

- *"Do not fear, for I am with you; Do not be afraid, for I am your God, I will strengthen you, I will also help you, I will also uphold you with My righteous right hand, behold, all those who are angered at*

> *you will be shamed and dishonored; Those who con-*
> *tend with you will be as nothing and will perish."*
> *Isaiah 41:10-11*

We can have complete confidence in victory over every encounter with darkness working through people or from within, if we take time with the Lord to be armed with His armor. "Love conquers all."

- *"Therefore, take up the full armor of God, so that you will be able to resist on the evil day, and having done everything, to stand firm. Stand firm therefore, having belted your waist with truth, and having put on the breastplate of righteousness; And having strapped on your feet the preparation of the gospel of peace;" Ephesians 6:13-15*

Taking up the armor of God to be ready and able to stand when darkness tries to deceive and destroy, begins with your focus and obedience to God's Holy Word. Having a clear understanding of the reason for your faith and a willingness to share it when the Holy Spirit leads is a powerful first step.

Please remember, peace should be the evidence that you are walking in the divine nature of Christ in you. A self-righteousness and judgmental attitude are evidence of sinful darkness misleading you. Pray and wait before God until you know in your heart, true surrender to Him. Now let's finish getting dressed in the armor.

- *"In addition to all, taking up the shield of faith with which you will be able to extinguish all the flaming arrows of the evil one. And take the helmet of salvation, and the sword of the Spirit, which is the word of God. With every prayer and request, pray at all times in the Spirit, and with this in view, be alert with all perseverance and every request for all the saints." Ephesians 6:16-18*

Putting on this armor is the same as developing a daily manner of life that is incorporated in "The Daily Walk" in this book. Knowing what you believe concerning the grace of God through Jesus Christ will protect you from thoughts and emotions that would be deceptive and destructive. Being able to think and speak the Word of God cuts the influence of darkness away from your mind and emotions and brings the peace of God. A constant attitude of prayer is very important for yourself as well as for all other believers. You are part of the body of Christ.

Questions to Ponder

1. Can you count on God in all circumstances?

- *"For the Lord is good; His mercy is everlasting and His faithfulness is to all generations." Psalms 100:5*

- *"No temptation has overtaken you except something common to mankind; and God is faithful, so He will not allow you to be tempted beyond what you are able, but with the temptation will provide the way of escape also, so that you will be able to endure it."* 1 Corinthians 10:13

(Many times, when trials and temptations seem to be getting the best of you, it is simply a sign you need to look to God and ask Him to help you tighten up the armor.)

2. Do you need be vulnerable any time during your walk with God?

- *"But thanks be to God, who always leads us in triumph in Christ, and through us reveals the fragrance of the knowledge of Him in every place."* 2 Corinthians 2:14

(Faithfully, in surrendering your will to God through humble, loving obedience, you become the recipient of the power and authority in the name of Christ through the presence of Christ in you.)

Be the Victor Not the Victim

You will find yourself wrestling with selfish desires at times. For your new divine nature to have victory you must rely on the divine authority that's been given to you in "Jesus' name." Using the authority, you have been given in Jesus' name, along with the effectiveness of claiming the truth of God's word over your thoughts and emotions, makes the authority and power of dark temptations fade and strengthens your divine nature.

- *"For the word of God is living, and active, and sharper than any two-edged sword, even penetrating as far as the division of soul and spirit, of both joints and marrow, and able to judge the thoughts and intentions of the heart."* Hebrews 4:12

Never underestimate the power of getting God's word in your thoughts to bring victory to your divine nature and have authority over your thoughts and emotions for your well-being.

Your spiritual door is now open. It may seem like old thought patterns and habits, and your divine nature are at war. You need to enter this journey knowing they are. The important thing to remember is, God is on your side, and you cannot lose, unless you accept less than He has for you.

- *"For the weapons of our warfare are not of the flesh, but divinely powerful for the destruction of fortresses. We are destroying arguments and all arrogance raised against the knowledge of God, and we*

> *are taking every thought captive to the obedience of Christ."* 2 Corinthians 10:4-5

Claiming and using the authority you have in the Name of Jesus and standing firmly in the knowledge of the Holy Spirit through God's word, will bring the fruit of the spirit forward from within you. This brings the discovery of spiritual treasures and strength in divine nature along this journey.

- *"But the fruit of the Spirit is love, joy, peace, patience, kindness, goodness, faithfulness, gentleness, self-control; against such things there is no law. Now those who belong to Christ Jesus crucified the flesh with its passions and desires."* Galatians 6:22-24

You may feel a little unsure what to do next. That is to be expected. You have a new divine nature to nurture and grow by learning to listen to and humbly follow the guidance of the Holy Spirit within you. He doesn't tap you on the shoulder and confirm his presence.

- *"For as he thinks within himself, so is he."* Proverbs 23:7

Your interests may change. You may take much greater joy in studying the Bible. You may desire to be around other believers as much as possible. Just be aware that your old thought patterns and habits may not immediately give way to the authority of your new divine nature. They have no authority over you now except what you allow them to have. The same goes for Satan and his helpers.

You may ask, how do I refuse to conform to their authority in everyday life and conform to the authority of my new divine nature? Always remember where the power and authority for your thoughts and emotions comes from now.

- *"And Jesus came up and spoke to them, saying, "all authority in heaven and on earth has been given to Me."* Mathew 28.18

- *"Behold, I have given you authority to walk on snakes and scorpions, and authority over all the power of the enemy, and nothing will injure you".* Luke 10:19

Remember this is spiritual power. Don't let ego squirm its way in your thoughts.

- *"Peace I leave with you, My peace I give you: not as the world gives, do I give to you. Do not let your hearts be troubled, nor fearful".* John 14:27

The power and peace are within you as a result of walking with Him through His word and prayer. When a worry or fear or if anything else comes up and causes turmoil in your mind and emotions, just know that darkness is trying to have its way, and your divine nature needs to be nourished in God's word and prayer by the Holy Spirit to take the authority you have been given. The result will be your divine nature growing in awareness of walking with God. When you prayerfully focus on God's word; Freedom, peace, and victory come to your mind and emotions.

- *"But the wisdom from above is first pure, then peace-loving, gentle, reasonable, full of mercy and good fruits, impartial, free of hypocrisy. And the fruit of righteousness is sown in peace by those who make peace."* James 3:17-18

Allow me to now give you the divine plan that will help you grow to a place you will not stumble. After the plan, I will give you the map to follow, in a committed daily walk, to grow in the mental and emotional freedom, that will result in accomplishing the plan though the daily walk. Remember: ego and pride play no part in the plan or the daily walk.

Questions to Ponder:

1. Now, with the invitation accepted, and the decision made, what is your responsibility in this relationship?

*   *"Seek the Lord and His strength; Seek His face continually."* Psalms 105:4

*   *"Ask, and it will be given to you; seek, and you will find; knock, and it will be opened to you."* Matthew 7:7

(When you do your part, exercising faith and believing, God will always do His. God's timing may be different than yours, but it is always for your good.)

2. God has a great plan for you, do you think He needs to tell you every detail of how to do your part each day?

(The great thing about God's plan for you is, each step you take in His plan, requires faith on your part. That strengthens your relationship with Him and brings heavenly rewards and transforms you. Any time spent before God changes you more and more. The important thing to remember is, His plan for you should not become complicated; It is, simply to walk with Him each day, where ever that may lead.)

The Divine Plan

This plan of action was given ages ago. It is practical and uncomplicated, simply requiring a sincere desire, and faith in God's assisting hand, for real, life-changing results. It is a plan that will have profound results regarding your thought and emotional wellbeing. This is the plan for growing in divine nature, an immovable foundation, to a place you will not stumble. This is a plan that gives direction to a daily walk of progression in your relationship with God.

This is a plan for aligning your thoughts, emotions, and actions with God's word, under the authority of your new divine nature in Christ. The rewards are for your life, now and eternally. "The Daily Walk" in this journey is designed to accomplish this plan as well as help keep you armed with the Spiritual armor of God.

- *"Grace and peace be multiplied to you in the knowledge of God, and of Jesus our lord, for His divine power has granted to us everything pertaining to life and godliness, through the true knowledge of Him who called us by His own glory and excellence. Through these He has granted to us His precious and magnificent promises, so that by them*

> *you may become partakers of the divine nature,*
> *having escaped the corruption that is in the world*
> *on account of lust."* 2 Peter 1:2-4

It is of utmost importance to not get caught in the trap of head knowledge at this point. To experience the divine power of God in Jesus our Lord, you have to answer His personal call and get to know Him, not just know of Him, otherwise you will not experience the divine promises which make you a partaker of the divine nature. Remember; *"God is spirit, and those who worship Him must worship in spirit and truth"* 1 John 4:24. The daily walk, is a stroll with God, to get to know Him more. He will enrich your knowledge and understanding of His riches of life in Christ along the way. To have the divine nature of Christ given to you, and not do what allows Him to be manifested through you, would be a tragedy.

- *"Now for this very reason also, applying all diligence, in your faith supply moral excellence, and in your moral excellence, knowledge, and in your knowledge, self-control, and in your self-control, perseverance, and in your perseverance, godliness, and in your godliness, brotherly kindness, and in your brotherly kindness, love. For if these qualities are yours and are increasing, they do not make you useless nor unproductive in the true knowledge of our Lord Jesus Christ."* 2 Peter 1:5-8

Now, here is your part in this divine plan. Notice each addition to your faith is brought about in the way you relate to others in daily life. Each of these qualities opens the way for Jesus to be seen in you and strengthens your personal knowledge of Him. I am not speaking of head knowledge; I am speaking of heart knowledge. Heart knowledge grows as Christ conforms you more and more in His image, as you add to your faith these character qualities of Himself. Take note that each day's conscious effort to add these personal qualities to your faith, is a daily step to greater freedom in Christ.

- *"For the one who lacks these qualities is blind or short-sighted, having forgotten his purification from his former sins. Therefore, brothers and sisters, be all the more diligent to make certain about His calling and choice of you; for as long as you practice these things, you will never stumble; for in this way the entrance into the eternal kingdom of our Lord and Savior Jesus Christ will be abundantly supplied to you."* 2 Peter 1:8-11

Now that you know, the goal of adding to your faith in Christ, will bring you to a place you will not stumble, I must tell you that the desires of the flesh are going to fight against your growth as well as Satan and his helpers. They will try to exert authority over your thoughts and feelings very subtly to lead you into doing or saying something that may seem very minor and unimportant. Just remember, every act of obedience to sin gives authority to your flesh, or Satan, which just leads to greater acts of enslavement.

- *"So, Jesus was saying to those Jews who had believed Him, if you continue in My word, then you are truly My disciples; and you will know the truth, and the truth will set you free."* John 8:31-32

"The Daily Walk", leads more and more, to freedom, from old thought patterns and deceptive emotions, to the dominion of your new divine nature in Christ. It will lead to daily victories and freedom and the divine promise of never stumbling. If this growth and maturity ever gets tainted with pride and ego, you can believe, that old, deceptive thought patterns and emotions are working against you. Remember, Satan and his helpers are very experienced at creating deceptive, and distracting thoughts and emotions. Claiming the peace of God over your mind and emotions, will bring you victory, in the battlefield of your mind, by submitting your army of thoughts to the arming of God's word, to guarantee a victory. Thus, learning to use God's Word, as the sword of the Spirit, will clear the field, for growth in faith and peace, in walking with God each day.

Questions to Ponder:

1. If you have confessed your belief in Christ, why do you need to add to your faith?

- *"If we say that we have fellowship with Him and yet walk in the darkness, we lie and do not practice the truth; but if we walk in the light as He Himself is in the light, we have fellowship with one another, and the blood of Jesus His son cleanses us from all sin."* 1 John 1:6-7

(God has told us how to be free and cleansed by the blood of Jesus from the things that bind us. Don't make the mistake of being deceived into thinking all you need is your free ticket to heaven so you can escape torment. Don't miss the journey of freedom and life for the sake of holding on to the old, deceptive, selfish, blind, sinful, influences of darkness.)

2. Is there a perfect example of someone who has had all these character qualities that you can look up to?

- *"But put on the Lord Jesus Christ, and make no provision for the flesh in regard to its lusts."* Romans 13:14

(When we add to our faith these qualities that lift us to a place where we will not stumble, we are putting on the Lord Jesus Christ and placing the authority of our life in His divine nature in us.)

A Good Mindset

When I was given the affirmations and verses that became "The Daily Walk" for me, I quoted them every morning and every night. I noticed a growing sense of peace and freedom that changed my view of everything and everyone. The greatest blessing, I have received on this daily walk, is a growing relationship with God, in Jesus Christ.

- *"Therefore, I urge you, brothers and sisters, by the mercies of God, to present your bodies as a living and holy sacrifice, acceptable to God, which is your spiritual service of worship. And do not be conformed to this world, but be transformed by the renewing of your mind, so that you may prove what the will of God is, that which is good and acceptable and perfect."* Romans 12:1-2

My time spent listening for the small, loving voice of guidance, of the Holy Spirit, has become a time of peace and loving respect, like learning from an eternal, trusted friend. I have been given a solid and unshakable mental, emotional, and spiritual foundation. Each day of the daily walk produces more worthy material to continue building on that foundation.

- *"But the Helper, the Holy Spirit whom the Father will send in My name, He will teach you all things, and remind you of all that I said to you."* John 14:26

As you continue allowing your divine nature in Christ to have authority over your thoughts, emotions, and actions on this daily walk, you will continue to receive the riches of God in Jesus Christ each step of the way.

- *"Behold, I have given you authority to walk on snakes and scorpions, and authority over all the power of the enemy, and nothing will injure you. Nevertheless, do not rejoice in this, that the spirits are subject to you, but rejoice that your names are recorded in heaven."* Luke 10:19-20

Take this daily walk under the authority of the divine nature of Christ, by the guidance of the Holy Spirit. Doing so means you can be victorious over the darkness of this world. Learning to exert that divine authority will come clearer each day. The name of Jesus and God's Holy Word are all powerful when it comes to wrestling with the darkness of this world. Don't get careless on this walk.

Remember our enemies are not flesh and blood. Don't allow them any influence over your thoughts or emotions.

Taking this daily walk is like placing treasures of gold and silver in the vault of your mind and heart which will yield dividends of peace and wisdom and understanding. This daily path will lead to adding to your faith the vital things that lift you in the divine nature of Christ where you will not stumble.

Walk this path with a humble, loving, obedient attitude under the guidance of the Holy Spirit through prayer and with a grateful, receptive heart. Watch daily for new understanding, victory, and freedom from binding thoughts and emotions.

After each verse and affirmation, I have shared a thought to help focus your deeper thinking and listening. Being in a quiet location, free of distractions, where you can focus and listen, will create a special time between you and God in which your eyes will be opened and your heart filled to overflowing. As you faithfully take this daily walk, may you become increasingly aware of God walking with you.

Questions to Ponder:

1. Is there any need to mentally or emotionally carry anything into this daily walk?

(The goal of the daily walk with God in Christ is to unburden yourself of mental and emotional burdens of the past, and find freedom and peace and maintain the same, through your ever-increasing ability to surrender to the authority of the divine nature of Christ in you.)

2. Is there an immediate effect to be expected through taking this walk?

(As you daily surrender, in a loving, obedient, and humble attitude, to the divine nature of Christ in you to guide you in receiving the truth and strength in the verses and affirmations, you will gain more and more wisdom and understanding that will make you truly free. The key thought to remember is, the divine nature of Christ in you, guided by the Holy Spirit, enables your walk with God each day. There is no other ground to take this daily walk. This is a spiritual walk, that will strengthen your heart (spirit), in taking authority over your thoughts, emotions, and flesh, to the glory of God, through Christ in you.)

Chapter Seven:

The Daily Walk

1. *"Watch over your heart with all diligence for from it flow the springs of life."* Proverbs 4:23

(Let this moment be the beginning of tending to your heart. You will be given the thoughts of life, freedom, and power to add to your faith moral excellence, knowledge, self-control, perseverance, godliness, brotherly kindness, and love. You will also learn to be mentally and spiritually equipped with God's armor to shield you and enable you to walk in daily victory. God's blessings be yours!)

2. *"For as he thinks within himself, so he is."* Proverbs 23:7

(Your mind is a powerful force to have operating for your good. You have the ability to determine which thoughts will have time on your mind.)

3. *"The good person out of the good treasure of his heart brings forth what is good; and the evil person out of the evil treasure brings forth what is evil: For his mouth speaks from that which fills his heart."* Luke 6:45

(Understanding what your words indicate about you will help you understand the expressions of others. You should examine your heart before opening your mouth. As the treasures of God build up in your heart, you share the wealth when you open our mouth.)

4. *"For with the heart a person believes, resulting in righteousness; and with the mouth he confesses, resulting in salvation."* Romans 10:10

(Sincere belief in Jesus Christ means true repentance, which means turning from your ways to follow God's will. That is the way of righteousness. Confessing is the divine nature of Christ in you being given the authority, by you, to free your flesh from the old, ingrained habits of thought and feeling that were borne from your old sinful human nature under the influences of darkness. Aligning your mouth, your mind, and your heart according to God's will fills the emptiness in your heart and brings true freedom. Regularly strengthen your abundance of heart with a clear confession and with true joy! Regular nurturing, in clearly confessing a growing belief, not only grows deep roots but also helps you rise to the level of your confession. Let your confession continue to grow in love, wisdom, truth, and joy.)

5. Today I will be totally pleased with the truth that I now have the divine nature of Christ in me. In any situation where my knowledge or experience fails to be impressive to myself or to others, I will accept the humbling fact of my imperfection and be thankful for my endless potential in Christ.

(Be joyfully aware, from now on, that life isn't all about you anymore; It's about Christ in you, for God's glory! There is no limit to God's goodness, so your potential is limitless!)

6. I will be pleased with who I am at the present, because of the divine nature of Christ in me, and fully accept the person the Lord is making of me.

(Taking this daily walk indicates that you are placing your life in God's hands to guide you in His will. He will always lift you higher and make you stronger in His love, joy, peace, wisdom, and understanding.)

7. I will always be ready to share my faith in Christ when the Lord provides the opportunity. Being a loving, overcoming, victorious instrument of the

Lord, in every circumstance, will be my greatest joy today.

(The message of the gospel of Christ is a loving, compassionate, gentle invitation to open the heart and receive the person of Jesus Christ as our Savior, Lord, and King, ultimately our heavenly High Priest. He brings gifts of unconditional love and forgiveness, the filling of His divine nature of life, the presence, teaching, and guidance of the Holy Spirit, and access to God our Father. He gives us the divine power and authority to overcome and to be free. This is only the beginning! Your heart condition will give power to your words. Keep it simple. It's a message of love, forgiveness, and life in Jesus Christ.)

8. I will continually focus my energy toward being totally given to the Lord, in mind, in effort, in relationships, wherever I might be.

(Making yourself constantly aware of the divine nature of the Son of God in you, strengthens your love in humble obedience to His guidance which is always for your good. *"And we know that God causes all things to work together for good to those who love God, for those who are called according to His purpose."* Romans 8:28. Know that you are called if you are on this Walk!)

9. I will never allow negative, destructive self-criticism to find a place in my mind. I will always seek to follow the guidance of my teacher, guide, and comforter; the Holy Spirit in me.

(Know that self-evaluation is not a guilt or shame producing activity to tear yourself down. It should be a time of confession and cleansing with God. *"If we confess our sins, He is faithful and righteous, so that He will forgive us our sins and cleanse us from all unrighteousness."* 1 John 1:9. Confession of sin, and repentance (turning from your ways to God's ways) brings God's cleansing power to action within you. No repentance brings guilt, shame, and helplessness.)

10. I will never allow fear to block any thoughts, words, or actions of obedience to the Lord.

(Stepping out in faith means overcoming fear. Just remember, your thoughts and emotions are vulnerable to the urges and false authority of your flesh and darkness of this world. Placing God's word in your mind gives authority to the divine nature of Christ in you to overcome and make you free of fear. Fear may not want to give you up easily. Don't give in! Taking the first step of faith, shrinks the challenge and dissolves its power over you, and opens your heart more to the joy of God being with you through all things.)

11. *"For God has not given us a spirit of timidity, but of power, and love, and discipline."* 2 Timothy 1:7

(When struggling with fear, simply profess God's Word, and the life that is in it will embolden and strengthen you to overcome.)

12. I will post a guard upon my mind to ward off any thoughts which may be destructive, guilt breeding, hateful, doubtful, evil, or that have any capacity in the least to cause disharmony in my mind or heart. I will have this thought stand guard on my mind: *"I have been crucified with Christ; And it is no longer I who live, but Christ lives in me; And the life which I now live in the flesh I live by faith in the Son of God, who loved me and gave Himself up for me."* Galatians 2:20

(Your mind is a powerful force in determining the way you feel, what you speak, what you do, and how you affect those around you. Don't take it for granted one more second. Protect it, and keep it headed in a growing, positive, powerful direction. Knowing you are not alone on this walk is a valuable mindset. Remind yourself regularly that Christ is your strength, and He is always present, by refocusing with this verse.)

13. I will not allow unkind words from others to create negative thoughts of myself.

(This is the perfect time to remind yourself of the helmet of salvation. You are a new person in Christ. Don't get deceived by misguided thoughts or emotions caused by someone or something else. Your old way of thinking or feeling may try to get wrapped up in a misguided adjustment. Your thoughts and emotions may move toward the traps of anger, vengefulness, guilt, or any number of deceptive traps. *"Therefore, if anyone is in Christ, this person is a new creation; the old things passed away; behold, new things have come."* 2 Corinthians 5:17. Give authority over your thoughts and emotions to your divine nature by getting God's word in your mind. That is the battleground. You will be victorious!)

14. I will not allow rejection of others to influence me to think of myself as unacceptable or unlikeable in any way.

(The breastplate of righteousness will protect your heart from these painful darts. The old thoughts and emotions seek for you to be accepted and approved of. The new divine nature of Christ in you assures you constantly of your divine acceptance and approval. *"The Lord is my light and my salvation; whom should I fear? The Lord is the defense of my life; whom should I dread?"* (Psalms 27:1) Use the Word of God to brush away such stinging darts of the heart. It is the sword of the spirit for you to use for your welfare, victory, and God's glory! Reaffirming your faith in Jesus Christ makes your walk with Him more personal and your faith becomes like a shield. It will protect you from being wounded because of the deceptive, and false influences of darkness over your mind and emotions.)

15. I will not allow angry thoughts to reside in my mind or breed hate and resentment.

(When anger takes root, it brings all kinds of negative influences to spring up. Don't allow it to get that far! Tend to your mind right away. "*Cast your burden upon the Lord and He shall sustain you; He will never allow the righteous to be shaken.*" Psalms 55:22)

16. I will not be influenced by anger to act or speak in any way that is hurtful or damaging at any time.

(Don't be moved to take action or speak from an emotional maladjustment of anger, because that is a surrender to the false authority of dark influences which is a path of enslavement. "*For sin shall not be master over you, for you are not under the law but under grace.*" Romans 6:14)

17. I will, by the ability God gives me, "*not be overcome by evil but overcome evil with good.*" Romans 12:21

(When you have the opportunity to overcome evil with good, selfishness will likely try to take you in a different direction. That is when it is evident that your strength will come to you, to do good, through prayer and humble obedience to God's word. Let love and wisdom have their way in you. You will be the overcomer.)

18. I will not allow my spirit to be crushed by any influence of this world, any person, or evil.

(When you feel week, insignificant, helpless, or broken, turning to God allows Him to show you how His power working in you can make you a new person. "*My grace is sufficient for you, for power is perfected in weakness.*" 2 Corinthians 12:9 "*Greater is He who is in you than he who is in the world.*" 1 John 4:4)

19. I will cultivate a solid courage and confidence in the abilities God gives me and the hope of salvation in Jesus my Lord in me.

(Focusing on God with you, in Christ, brings the courage and confidence needed for any occasion, anytime, anywhere. "*But thanks be to God, who always leads us in triumph in Christ, and through us reveals the fragrance of the knowledge of Him in every place.*" 2 Corinthians 2:14. Just be confident in the power of God in Christ being with you always through faith. It is not reserved for a future event; it is yours now!)

20. "*I can do all things through Him who strengthens me.*" Philippians 4:13

(Rest assured that whatever God leads you to do in Christ, He will enable you to do. Whatever the task may be will not exhaust you, but it will make you stronger.)

21. "*Greater is He who is in you than he who is in the world.*" John 4:4

(Making yourself aware of the presence of the Lord in you is one of the greatest practices of faith that you can do. "*These things I have spoken to you so that in Me you may have peace. In the world you have tribulation, but take courage; I have overcome the world.*" John 16:33.)

22. "*If God is for us, who is against us?*" Romans 8:31

(You can always count on God's love and faithfulness. "*For the Lord is good; His mercy is everlasting and His faithfulness is to all generations.*" Psalms 100:5)

23. "*But in all these things we overwhelmingly conquer through Him who loved us.*" Romans 8:37

(The law of the spirit supersedes the law of sin and death. Everyone is borne under the law of sin and death which is binding and condemning and blinding in its limitations. The victory Christ has won over the law of sin and death is translated to your life in everything when you walk with Christ in you. "*Therefore, there is now no condemnation at all for those who are in Christ Jesus. For the law of the Spirit of life in Christ Jesus has set you free from the law of sin and death. For the mind set on the flesh is death, but the mind set on the Spirit is life and peace.*" Romans 8:1, 2, 6. The effect this walk has on your thoughts and emotions is eternally important.)

24. I will face all this day has in it with confidence, courage, and hope, in the power and faith in Christ who dwells within me.

(Whatever this day may have in store for you, set your mind for victory first thing. "*Do not be anxious about anything, but in everything by prayer and pleading with thanksgiving let your requests be made known to God. And the peace of God, which surpasses all comprehension, will guard your hearts and minds in Christ Jesus,*" Philippians 4:6-7. It was meant from the beginning for your mind and emotions to be influenced by God for your good.)

25. "*Search me, God, and know my heart; Put me to the test and know my anxious thoughts; And see if*

there is any hurtful way in me, and lead me in the way everlasting." Psalms 139:23-24

(Speaking to God in an attitude of surrender and humble obedience will open the way for God's guidance in preventing you from being an unwilling victim of the darkness in the world.)

26. *"Do not fear for I am with you; Do not be afraid, for I am your God. I will strengthen you; I will also help you. I will also uphold you with my righteous right hand."* Isaiah 41:10

(This is a wonderfully powerful promise to claim when facing a challenge that may seem overwhelming. Reclaiming this promise all through the day, even without a challenge, is a great way to secure the armor of God, girding yourself with the Word.)

27. *"But we have this treasure in earthen containers, so that the extraordinary greatness of the power will be of God and not from ourselves."* 2 Corinthians 4:7

(Do not let prideful, or selfish thoughts and emotions deceive you when God does something special through you. Always give thankful credit and praise to God for His guidance and the abilities He gives you by His presence with you.)

28. *"The reward of humility and the fear of the Lord are riches, honor, and life.* Proverbs 22:4

(Keeping a humble attitude of obedience and loving reverence toward God in Jesus Christ has wonderful rewards. Do not seek the rewards; seek the relationship which brings the rewards.)

29. I will seek God's guidance through His word and prayer, for all my life's circumstances.

(Do not assume that God will intervene in everything without your seeking His face. He knows we all will easily stray and take Him for granted until we don't even have a thought of Him. Nurturing your relationship with Him through His word and prayer will keep you on the path of obedience and humble gratitude and will open your circumstances to His power in Christ, in you.)

30. I will pray daily, for all God's people, for we are all connected through faith in Jesus Christ as our Lord and Savior, King, and High Priest.

(Carrying out your basic calling, to pray for all God's people, will cultivate blessings of God's power working in others, and you, to strengthen the body in the working of God's will.)

Questions to Ponder

1. Did any verse or affirmation stand out to you, indicating the possible need for further prayer and study?

2. Do you have any individual concern that may present a need for you to add your own verse or affirmation for your daily renewed focus?

Post Walk Considerations

Nurture your mind and heart with these verses and affirmations each day, and just see the affect they will have in your life. When facing a fearful challenge or when the odds seem strongly against you, just refresh your mind by focusing on any of these verses or affirmations that can erase fear and doubt and let the peace of God have its way. You can also add any verses or affirmations that give more strength and faith in your life situation. There is power in just focusing on the name of Jesus in the midst of troubles. Keep it simple. When stuck in a condition of indecision, just get in the condition of surrendering to God, and allow Him to lead by His wisdom and understanding, and you will never be disappointed. Whatever He sets before you, He will enable you to do.

Mental Discipline

During the daily routine of earning a living, traveling, meeting with others, or just basically anything, our thoughts are inclined to take whatever direction they may be pulled in. That could be like following our pet dog wherever it wanders off to until we find ourselves in the middle of a situation, and we have to make distracting adjustments. Just a little direction and effort can get us in the habit of guiding our thoughts in the proper direction to create the emotional condition that promotes wellbeing:

- *"Do not be anxious about anything, but in everything by prayer and pleading with thanksgiving let your requests be made known to God. And the peace of God, which surpasses all comprehension, will guard your hearts and minds in Christ Jesus. Finally, brothers and sisters, whatever is true, whatever is honorable, whatever is right, whatever is pure, whatever is lovely, whatever is commendable, if there is any excellence and if anything, worthy of praise, think about these things."* Philippians 4:6-8

If you feel uneasy or drawn in the direction of any negative or disruptive thought or emotion, it is a clear indication that the flesh is trying to have its way. That is the time to trust the still, small, voice within that will guide you away from the distracting trap that you may be headed for.

- *"I will instruct you and teach you in the way which you should go; I will advise you with my eye upon you."* Psalms 32:8

Priceless Awareness

This is a journey that God has set before "you". That is because God has specific gifts meant for you, to enrich your life as well as those around you, by guiding you in living a life of freedom and victory, through the divine nature of Christ in you. The possibilities are endless.

The beginning of such a loving, priceless friendship with our Lord can be stopped in its tracks quickly if daily distractions take your attention away from Him. You have to realize that you are in a continuing state of repentance (seeking God's ways above our own).

When you decide to think, feel, or do something that is not according to God's will, you can become aware of a sense of shame or guilt. It is very important to know that this is the time to confess and repent, to keep your walk with God each day from becoming distant and impersonal. Confessing a sin before God and repenting (turning from it) brings God's help to you.

- *"If we confess our sins, he is faithful and righteous, so that He will forgive us our sins and cleans us from all unrighteousness."* 1 John 1:9

Keeping your daily walk with God personal and unhindered will be life changing and enriching with endless potential.

There are many things you can do to keep your focus trained on His presence with you. A very important attitude to cultivate is a prayerful awareness of His presence.

- *"Trust in the Lord with all your heart and do not lean on your own understanding. In all your ways acknowledge Him, and He will make your paths straight."* Proverbs 3:5-6

It is also a great blessing to have someone to discuss any questions that may come up along the way. It is very beneficial and important to attend a good church regularly to be involved in Bible study groups. It also helps to be around like-minded believers to encourage each other in adding to your faith, the character of Christ, as described in "The Plan".

God Equips

The Lord gives many gifts to equip His people for certain loving tasks. When God puts something on your heart to do, you may feel you are totally unqualified to do it. He is wanting you to step out in faith and trust in His qualifications to work in you and through you for His glory. The blessings are endless if you step out by faith when He prompts. Living in the victory and authority of the divine nature of Christ is the result of walking by faith.

- *"And He gave some as apostles, some as prophets; some as evangelists, some as pastors and teachers, for the equipping of the saints for the work of the ministry, for the building up of the body of Christ; until we all attain to the unity of the faith, and of the knowledge of the Son of God, to a mature man, to the measure of the stature which belongs to the fullness of Christ."* Ephesians 4:11-13

He has given everything needed to build up the body of Christ (all believers). The goal is the unity of the faith, the knowledge of the Son of God, and to maturity into the fulness of Christ. This all builds the kingdom of God by the authority given to us in Christ, for the glory of God. Notice there is no mention of having a pass that grants passage into Heaven at some future time. This is not about gaining passage to a place. This is all about building a relationship as a body, with Christ, to the glory of God.

- *"As a result we are no longer to be children, tossed here and there by waves and carried about by every*

> *wind of doctrine, by the trickery of people, by crafti-
> ness in deceitful scheming; but speaking the truth in
> love, we are to grow up in all aspects into Him who is
> the head, that is, Christ, from whom the whole body,
> being fitted and held together by what every joint
> supplies, according to the proper working of each
> individual part, causes the growth of the body for
> the building up of itself in love."* Ephesians 4:14-16

Speaking the truth in love allows for our growth from spiritual childhood to maturity in Christ. The foundation for such a growing body is established already in the unconditional love and humble obedience of Christ making a way for us all to grow together. Our growing into the fullness of Christ has been conditioned on doing it as a body. Let each of us walk by loving faith as part of the body of Christ which opens the way for the power of God through each one to raise us all closer to God. It takes time and patience for each one of us to learn our potential within the body of Christ. Most of all, it takes loving, humble, faithful obedience in Christ.

Allow me to tell you about a man that has meant a great deal to me. I fortunately met him soon after my journey began, and his council and wisdom made a world of difference to me. His name is DD Paul Beran. I would recommend to anyone on this journey to pray for a mentor to discuss any questions that may come up and have a prayer with occasionally.

A Continuous Prayer

My standing prayer is for you, and everyone that picks this book up, to be on this magnificent daily walk.

1. Walking with the full assurance of what Jesus Christ has done, for you, is doing within you, and will do through you, to the glory of God, in the power of the Holy Spirit.

2. Joyfully witnessing daily, what Jesus is doing in you and through you.

3. Daily, becoming more aware of being filled and guided by His divine nature, within you.

4. Maintaining the thoughts and emotions that promote a life that only God can give:

- *"We are taking every thought captive to the obedience of Christ"*. *2* Corinthians 10:5.

- *"Do not let your heart be troubled; believe in God, believe also in me"*. John 14:1.

God guide you and bless you greatly!

CPSIA information can be obtained
at www.ICGtesting.com
Printed in the USA
JSHW080758280523
42150JS00002BA/11